The Strategic Marketing Process

How to Structure Your Marketing Activities to Achieve Better Results

Second Edition – 2013

STRATEGY

TOOLS

CUSTOMER
ACQUISITION

Written by Moderandi Inc., creators of the marketing planning and management app at www.MarketingMO.com

The Strategic Marketing Process

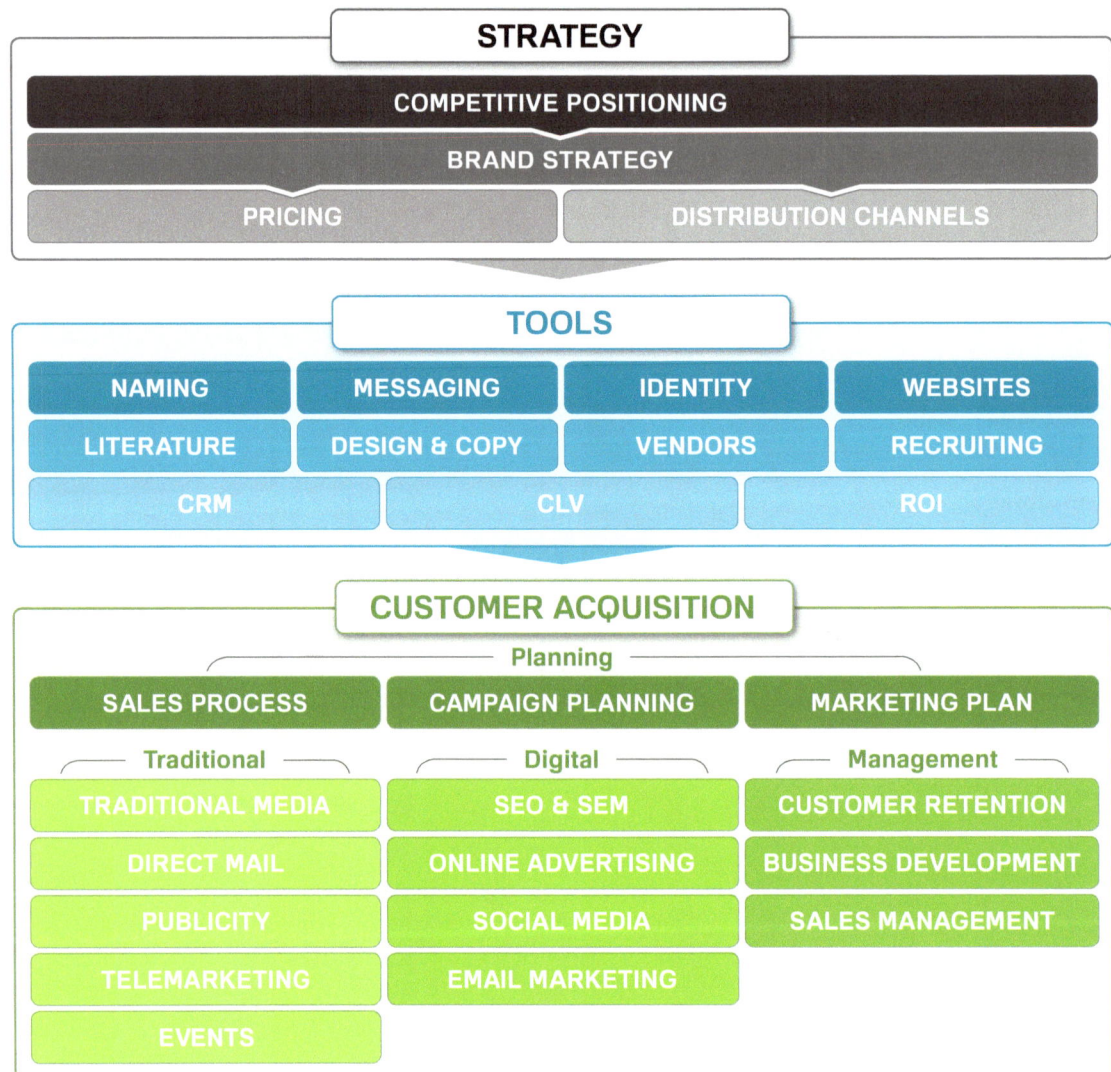

STRATEGY

COMPETITIVE POSITIONING

BRAND STRATEGY

| PRICING | DISTRIBUTION CHANNELS |

TOOLS

NAMING	MESSAGING	IDENTITY	WEBSITES
LITERATURE	DESIGN & COPY	VENDORS	RECRUITING
CRM	CLV	ROI

CUSTOMER ACQUISITION

Planning

| SALES PROCESS | CAMPAIGN PLANNING | MARKETING PLAN |

Traditional	Digital	Management
TRADITIONAL MEDIA	SEO & SEM	CUSTOMER RETENTION
DIRECT MAIL	ONLINE ADVERTISING	BUSINESS DEVELOPMENT
PUBLICITY	SOCIAL MEDIA	SALES MANAGEMENT
TELEMARKETING	EMAIL MARKETING	
EVENTS		

This guide was written by the team at Moderandi Inc., creator of the Marketing MO™ planning and management web app.

Marketers use our app to:

› Create plans in 3 clicks for over 300 common marketing activities

› Receive step-by-step guidance for each subject covered in this guide

› Organize and manage their marketing activities

If you like this guide, feel free to dig deeper at www.MarketingMO.com.

ISBN Print: 978-0-9887431-0-6

Introduction

"It was the best of times, it was the worst of times . . ."

Charles Dickens, *A Tale of Two Cities*

The Internet has fundamentally changed the marketing function, causing the greatest shift in the field since the invention of the television.

Digital marketing, social media and mobile devices have dramatically changed how we connect with our audiences. They've created a tremendous opportunity, as well as a tremendous burden.

The marketing function has become complicated.

No longer can we rely on print, publicity and a media buyer to distribute our catchy ad campaign; marketing nowadays requires heavy IT resources and an understanding of complex metrics to effectively (and profitably) connect with our market—busier people, who have shorter attention spans, and often suffer from information overload.

Social media, search engine marketing, email marketing, mobile devices, website optimization, content marketing . . . it's impossible for an individual marketer to master them all, *in addition* to their traditional media activities. And then there's strategic planning, creative development and financial measurement.

It's overwhelming. And it has caused many marketers to specialize, focusing on a single medium as their area of expertise.

But the reality in most small to mid-size enterprises (SMEs) is that their marketing team only has room for a handful of specialists, if any. Most don't have the budget to employ experts in all the necessary marketing mediums needed to effectively reach their audience. And even if they do have the budget, they often don't have enough work to justify hiring full-time specialists.

If you're not a specialist hired solely for your expertise, you're forced to know a little about a lot—to be well-versed in how to use a combination of digital and traditional mediums to effectively meet your revenue goals.

For the typical marketer at an SME, it's created a quandary:

  Identifying the "right things" to be doing, and then learning how to do them well

Many would argue that it's more difficult for marketers to determine *what* we should be doing, instead of how to do things right.

If we're not sure what we should be doing, it's easy to dive into the hot new *tactic of the moment* . . . without having a strong understanding of how it ties into the rest of our revenue-generation activities.

Specialization makes it easier to perform tactics well, but specialists aren't necessarily the best resource to determine strategy—the "right things" to be doing. Specialists typically favor their own area of expertise.

The 30,000-Foot Approach

This guide defines a marketing process that you can use to put structure around your daily, monthly and annual revenue-generating activities. It will help you gain a better understanding of what you should be doing, and how it fits into your overall strategy and departmental activities.

The guide groups common activities into three buckets, to clarify how the activities fit together in the revenue-generation process:

› **Strategy:** Your high-level conceptualization of how your offering will penetrate your market. This is your global, long-term, go-to-market strategy, and it may cover 5 to 10 years.

› **Tools:** The collateral, assets, software and processes that you use during the tactical execution of your strategies.

› **Customer Acquisition:** The marketing mediums and tactics that you use to execute your strategies to achieve your goals.

Visualizing these buckets helps to reinforce the need for strategy before tactics. Search engine marketing is a marketing medium in the customer acquisition bucket. It's not a strategy—it's a tactic, supported by tools (your website, sales literature, messaging, etc.), which should be tied to a strategy.

Our process covers more than just traditional marketing and ties together all go-to-market business activities: strategic planning, financial planning and measurement, creative development, marketing execution and sales, and customer retention.

Since marketing is always evolving, don't shy away from subjects and ideas that are new. Good marketers are always learning.

Embrace marketing, and most importantly, enjoy creating value for your market and communicating the value of your activities to your team.

SHARE
this ebook:

Table of Contents

Competitive Positioning

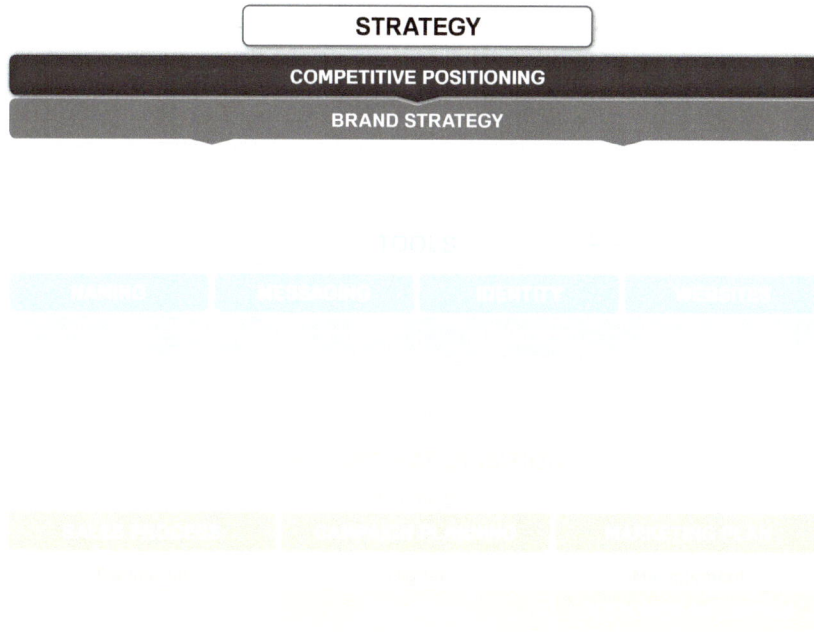

STRATEGY

COMPETITIVE POSITIONING

BRAND STRATEGY

What sets your product, service or company apart from your competitors? What value do you provide and how is it different from the alternatives?

Competitive positioning is about defining how you'll differentiate your offering and create value for your market. It's about carving out a spot in the competitive landscape, putting your stake in the ground, and winning mindshare in the marketplace—being known for a certain "something."

A good positioning strategy is influenced by:

› **Market profile:** Size, competitors, stage of growth
› **Customer segments or personas:** Groups of prospects with similar wants & needs
› **Competitive analysis:** Strengths, weaknesses, opportunities and threats in the landscape
› **Method for delivering value:** How you deliver value to your market at the highest level

When your market clearly sees how your offering is different from that of your competition, it's easier to influence the market and win mindshare. Without differentiation, it takes more time and budget to entice the market to engage with you; as a result, many companies end up competing on price—a tough position to sustain over the long term.

One of the key elements that many small to mid-size companies overlook is how they provide value at the highest level. There are three essential methods for delivering value: operational excellence, product leadership and customer intimacy.

Here is a hypothetical example of each:

Operational Excellence	Product Leadership	Customer Intimacy
Herringer customers don't want bells and whistles; they just want a good product at the lowest possible price. Herringer focuses on operational excellence so they can continually offer the lowest price in the market. For example, they just patented a new machine that dramatically lowers their manufacturing costs. They're not trying to create new or better products; they just want to produce more volume at a lower cost. Herringer's method for delivering value is operational excellence; it's a key driver of their long-term strategy, and their positioning reflects it.	Orange Technology's customers care most about quality—they want the best product. Orange is completely dedicated to innovation and quality. They're constantly working on product improvements and new ideas to bring to market. They know what their competitors are doing and are completely focused on staying one step ahead in order to capture a greater share of their market. Orange's brand and culture is all about product leadership; their market recognizes it and is willing to pay for it.	Starboard's market is flooded with products at all points of the price spectrum. Yet, Starboard's customers want more than a product off the shelf; they want customized solutions. So Starboard's strategy is to know as much as possible about their customers' businesses so they can deliver the correct solutions over time. Starboard knows that they can't just say "We offer great service." Starboard delivers on their strategy in every interaction with their market.

These companies have a complete understanding of how they deliver value to their market. It's part of their strategy, which makes it easier for them to win a position in their respective markets.

Here's another way to think of it:

You can provide the best offering, the cheapest offering, or the most comprehensive offering, but you *can't provide all three.*

Another key factor in your positioning is your competition. Sure, you need to put your stake in the ground and claim your turf. But is it turf that you can own? Can you realistically beat your competition to own it?

Rather than leaving your market positioning to chance, establish a strategy. What you're ultimately striving for is to be known for something—to own mindshare of the market. This is typically easier for consumer product lines than for B2B companies, because positioning a single product against three to five competitors is a simpler task than positioning a mid-size B2B company with numerous offerings in numerous markets.

Owning a strong position in the market is challenging for most small- to mid-size companies, but you have a better chance of achieving it if you clearly define a strategy and build your brand around it.

SHARE
this ebook:

Do you see your company in any of these scenarios?

Best Case	Neutral Case	Worst Case
You provide a one-of-a-kind offering that your market needs and wants; you have strong differentiation from your competitors. Your market knows your name and associates it with that "one thing" that you're known for. And you continually deliver on it—perception is reality—so you continue to win mindshare in your market, defending your turf and influencing your market.	Your offering is somewhat different from—and better than—those of your competitors, and you communicate that difference (though probably not as consistently as you should). Some of your market knows your name, but they describe you in different ways; you're not yet known for that "one thing," but at least you're occasionally recognized. You know that you could make a greater impact on your market with stronger positioning.	Your market sees little difference between you and your competitors, and your name is not recognized. Because of this, you have to spend precious budget and time educating the market at each touch point. You often end up competing solely on price, though your business isn't optimized to continue profitably with falling prices. You have to fight long and hard for every sale. It's very difficult to meet your revenue and profit goals.

How Competitive Positioning Aligns with Strategy

The concept of positioning is entirely strategic. It's the first element to address in strategic marketing, and everything else is aligned to it. Jack Trout and Al Ries defined the concept years ago in their landmark book Positioning: The Battle for Your Mind.

While the concept is simple—to be known for a single thing in the mind of the customer—the road to achieve it can be complex. It's best to have a clear understanding of your market—demographics, segments, their pains, how well you and your competitors provide solutions, how you truly provide value, and your strengths and weaknesses—before making this decision.

A fully-informed decision is vital, because you'll allocate a significant amount of resources in your journey to achieve it.

Key Concepts & Steps

Profile your market

› Document the size of your market.

› Identify your major competitors and how they're positioned.

› Determine whether your market is in the introductory, growth, mature, or declining stage of its life. This "lifecycle stage" affects your strategy.

Segment your market

› Understand the problems that your market faces. Talk with prospects and customers, or conduct research if you have the time, budget and opportunity. Uncover their true wants and needs—you'll learn a great deal about what you can deliver to solve their problems and beat your competitors.

› Group your prospects into "segments" or "personas" that have similar problems and can use your offering in similar ways. By grouping prospects into segments or personas, you can efficiently market to each group.

Define how you deliver value

› At the highest level, there are three core types of value that a company can deliver: operational efficiency (the lowest price), product leadership (the best product), or customer intimacy (the best solution & service). Determine which one you're best equipped to deliver; your decision is your method for delivering value.

Evaluate your competition

› List your competitors. Include any that can solve your customers' problems, even if the competitors' solutions are much different from yours—they're still your competition.

› Rate yourself and your direct competitors based on operational efficiency (price), product leadership and customer intimacy. It's easy to think you're the best, so be as impartial as you can be.

Stake a position

› Identify areas where your competition is vulnerable.

› Determine whether you can focus on those vulnerable areas—they're major opportunities.

› Make a decision on how to position your offering or company.

Select the mindshare you want to own, and create your strategy to achieve it

› Review the components of your market and evaluate what you want to be known for in the future. Condense all your research and analysis into the "one thing" that you want to be known for, and design your long-term strategy to achieve it.

Next Steps

Develop a brand strategy to help you communicate your positioning and solidify your value every time you touch your market. Together, these two strategies are the essential building blocks for your business.

SHARE
this ebook:

Brand Strategy

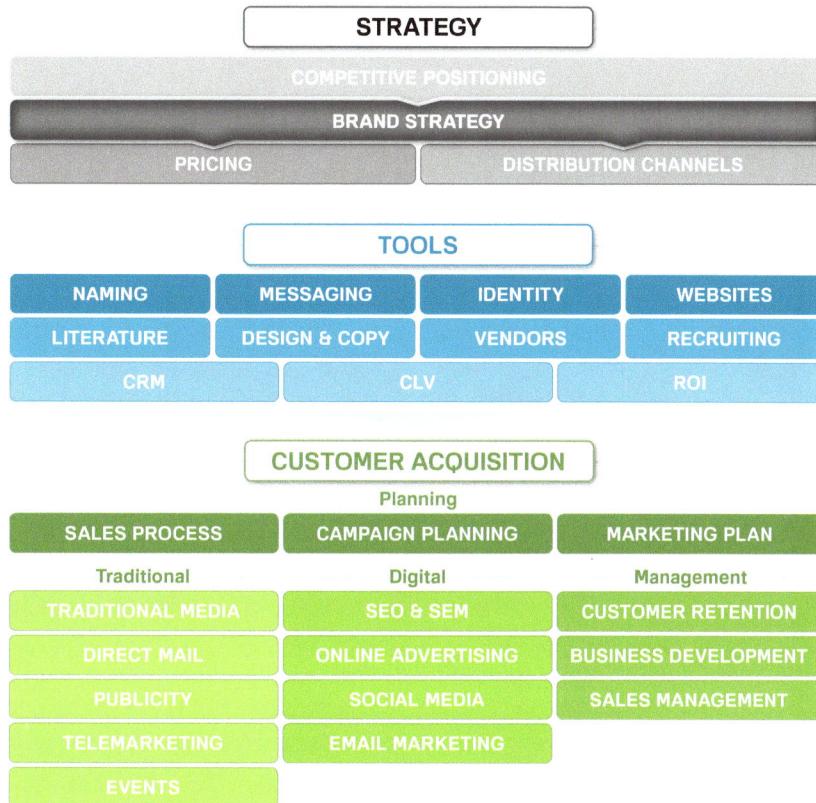

STRATEGY		
COMPETITIVE POSITIONING		
BRAND STRATEGY		
PRICING	DISTRIBUTION CHANNELS	

TOOLS			
NAMING	MESSAGING	IDENTITY	WEBSITES
LITERATURE	DESIGN & COPY	VENDORS	RECRUITING
CRM	CLV	ROI	

CUSTOMER ACQUISITION

Planning

SALES PROCESS	CAMPAIGN PLANNING	MARKETING PLAN

Traditional	Digital	Management
TRADITIONAL MEDIA	SEO & SEM	CUSTOMER RETENTION
DIRECT MAIL	ONLINE ADVERTISING	BUSINESS DEVELOPMENT
PUBLICITY	SOCIAL MEDIA	SALES MANAGEMENT
TELEMARKETING	EMAIL MARKETING	
EVENTS		

How do you define a brand? Is it a logo, a name or a slogan, or a graphic design or a color scheme?

Your brand is the entire experience that your market has with your offering or company. It's what you stand for, a promise that you make, and the personality that you convey.

And while it includes your logo, your color palette and your slogan, these are only creative elements that convey your brand. In reality, your brand lives in the day-to-day interactions you have with your market:

› The images you convey

› The messages you deliver on your website and in your campaigns

› The way your employees interact with customers

› A customer's opinion of you versus your competition

Branding is crucial for products and services sold in huge consumer markets. It's also important in B2B because it helps you stand out from your competition. It brings your competitive positioning to life; it defines you as a certain "something" in the mind of your market.

Think about successful consumer brands like Apple, Disney or Starbucks. You probably know what each brand represents. Now imagine that you're competing against one of these brands. If you want to capture significant market share, start with a strong positioning and brand or you won't be successful.

If you're B2C, it's likely that a few brands dominate your market. If you're B2B, there may or may not be a strong brand in your market. But when you put two companies up against each other, the one that represents something valuable and memorable will have an easier time reaching, engaging, and converting customers. It's a perception—and for most, perception equals reality.

Successful branding creates "brand equity"—the amount of money that customers are willing to pay just because it's your brand. Brand equity is an intangible asset that can be tracked on your balance sheet, and can make your company more valuable over the long term.

Instead of allowing your market to brand you, strive to have their experience with your brand align with your strategy.

Best Case	Neutral Case	Worst Case
Your market recognizes your name, knows exactly what you deliver, and you're known for that certain "something" in their mind. You deliver a consistent experience that the market has come to expect, both visually and operationally, at every market interaction. Customer acquisition happens quickly because your brand influences your market.	The market may not have a consistent view or impression of your offering, but you think that it's positive overall. You haven't thought a lot about branding because it doesn't seem necessarily relevant, but you admit that you can do a better job of communicating consistently with the market. You're not helping yourself, but you're not hurting yourself either.	You don't have a brand strategy and it shows. It's more difficult to communicate with your market and convince them to buy. They don't have a clear impression of your offering or why it's better. What you do, what you say, and how you say it, may contradict each other and confuse your market. Competitors who communicate effectively have a better shot at winning customers.

How Brand Strategy Aligns with Strategy

At its title suggests, brand strategy is completely strategic; it's your plan for how to achieve your desired positioning—how to become known for that certain "something." It describes the consistent experience that you desire to deliver to your market at each touch point.

Key Concepts & Steps

Audit your existing brand

› If you have an existing brand, conduct a survey of your market and your stakeholders to understand how they view your brand. This will give you an understanding of where you are and how much work needs to be done to get to where you want to be.

› Before creating your survey, outline what you think your brand should stand for, so you have criteria to evaluate against the responses. If you're not sure how to create your brand criteria, complete the next steps, and then conduct your audit.

Define your brand architecture

› Evaluate the features and benefits of your product / service. A feature is an attribute—a color, a configuration; a benefit is what that feature does for the customer.

› Identify which benefits are emotional (instead of functional)—the most powerful brand strategies tap into emotions, even among business buyers.

› Review the emotional benefits and boil them down to your brand pillars—the three things that your brand should mean to your market.

SHARE
this ebook:

Define your brand experience

› Think of your brand as a person with a distinct personality. Describe him or her, and then convey these traits in everything that you do and create.

› Determine your brand promise—the one thing that you deliver each time you interact with your market.

Write your brand story and positioning statement

› Write your 25-word positioning statement that conveys the essence of your brand. It conveys who you are, what you do, for whom, and one or two emotional benefits from interacting with your brand. Use it throughout your marketing materials.

› Write your brand story. This should convey your personality, your purpose—the difference that you're trying to make with your product, service or company. It builds credibility, differentiates you from your competition, and gives the market a reason to listen to you. Seth Godin says that the two elements that must come together in a brand story are:

  › The story you can confidently tell

  › The worldview the buyer tells herself

When those align, you win.

Define your brand visual and operational requirements

› Choose colors, fonts and other visual elements that match your personality.

› Determine how your employees will interact with your market to convey your personality and ensure your brand "lives" within your company.

Next Steps

Together with your competitive positioning strategy, your brand strategy is the essence of what you represent. A great brand strategy helps you communicate more effectively with your market, so be true to it in every interaction you have with your prospects and customers.

For example, you'll reinforce your brand strategy through your pricing, your distribution channels, your name and corporate identity, your messages, your literature, your website and your marketing campaigns.

Pricing

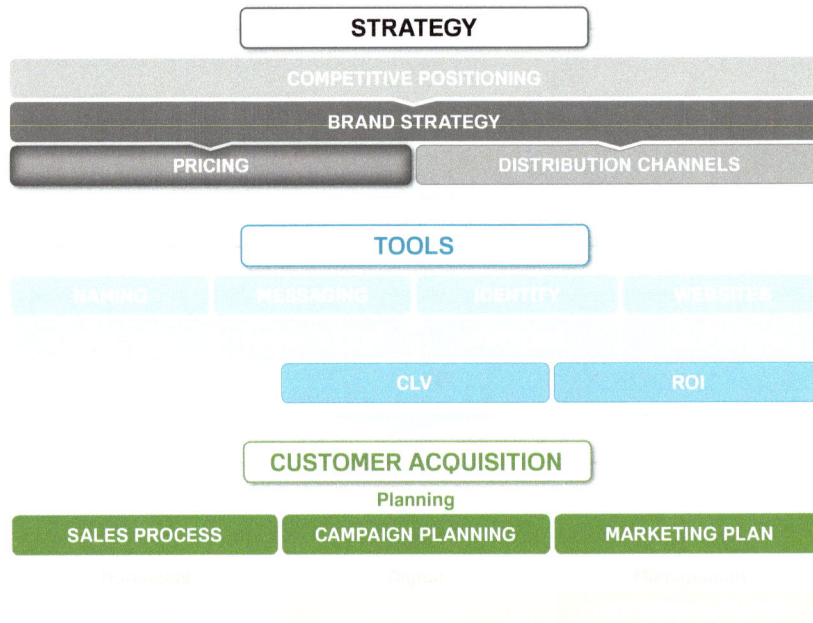

STRATEGY

COMPETITIVE POSITIONING

BRAND STRATEGY

PRICING | DISTRIBUTION CHANNELS

TOOLS

NAMING | MESSAGING | IDENTITY | WEBSITES

CLV | ROI

CUSTOMER ACQUISITION

Planning

SALES PROCESS | CAMPAIGN PLANNING | MARKETING PLAN

Price is one of the classic "4 Ps" of marketing (product, price, place, promotion). Since price is one of the 4Ps, it's a key element of every B2C marketing strategy. Yet in many B2B companies, marketers aren't involved in pricing strategy.

Pricing is a complex subject—there are many factors to consider, both short- and long-term. For example, your prices need to:

› Reflect the value that you provide versus your competitors

› Consider what the market will truly pay for your offering

› Enable you to reach your revenue and market share goals

› Maximize your profits (either short-term or long-term)

When you have a truly unique offering with little direct competition, it can be challenging to establish your price. Create a competitive analysis and strong strategy to understand:

› What your prospects might pay for other solutions to their problems

› Where your price should fall in relation to theirs

When your pricing, positioning, brand strategy and distribution channels are aligned, you're in the best situation to maximize revenue and profits.

SHARE
this ebook:

Do you see your company in one of these scenarios?

Best Case	Neutral Case	Worst Case
Company A provides a premium product, sold through carefully-selected retail outlets. Their pricing is typically 15% above the competition—they're the most expensive product in their class. Their demand curve is relatively inelastic, meaning that their market isn't that sensitive to price. Much of that results from the carefully selected positioning and branding over the past five years. Company A's products never go on sale, and retailers strictly adhere to pricing rules and brand guidelines.	Company B charges an average price for an average product. When they're behind their sales targets, individual reps are given the green light to discount if needed to meet their sales quotas. Management doesn't want to get in a price war, but is willing to ensure that they hit their short-term numbers. Management knows that they could spend more in R&D to differentiate their offering and have greater pricing power, but they haven't yet committed the budget to do so.	Company C provides business consulting services. To grow, they drop their hourly rates by up to 40%. This gives them access to an entire new set of clients. Low rates mean they can't afford the same top-tier consulting talent. The quality of their offering suffers, and they end up providing mediocre service for both markets. By lowering the price of their "prestige" brand to access a new market, Company C has increased its revenue, while reducing its profit margin and damaging its brand.

How Pricing Aligns with Strategy

It's best to define your positioning, create your brand strategy, and identify your distribution channels before you develop your pricing strategy. By doing so, you'll ensure that your pricing reflects your value and reinforces your brand.

For example, if your method for delivering value is product leadership, you shouldn't discount heavily or compete on price; you should also minimize pricing conflicts with any channel partners.

Your pricing influences how the market perceives your offering. If you're perceived as a commodity, you must either change the market's perception via a new positioning strategy, or compete on price and focus on innovating to keep costs low so you can still make a profit.

Key Concepts & Steps

Align your pricing strategy to your method for delivering value

Your price sends a strong message to your market—it needs to be consistent with the value you're delivering.

› If your method for delivering value is operational efficiency, then your price needs to be extremely competitive.

› If your method for delivering value is product leadership or customer intimacy, a low price sends the wrong message. After all, if a luxury item isn't expensive, is it really a luxury?

Understand your cost structure and profitability goals

Companies calculate these costs differently, so verify the exact calculations your company uses for:

› **Cost of goods sold (COGS):** the cost to physically produce a product or service

› **Gross profit:** the difference between the revenue you earn on a product and the cost to physically produce it

In addition, understand how much profit the company needs to generate. With this knowledge, you'll be far more effective when considering discount promotions—you'll know exactly how low you can go and still be profitable.

Analyze your competitors' prices

Look at a wide variety of direct and indirect competitors to gauge where your price falls. If your method for delivering value is operational efficiency, evaluate your competitors on a regular basis to ensure that you remain competitive.

Determine price sensitivity

A higher price typically means lower volume. Yet you may generate more total revenue and/or profit with fewer units at the higher price; it depends on how sensitive your customers are to price fluctuations. If they're extremely sensitive, you may be better off at a much lower price with substantially greater volume.

Estimate how sensitive your customers are to fluctuations—it will help you determine the right price and volume combination. More importantly, you can estimate how a price change can impact your revenue.

Next Steps

Once you've finalized your pricing strategy, you can review your tools to make sure they support your strategy. Then, dive into your sales process and campaign planning.

SHARE
this ebook:

Distribution Channels

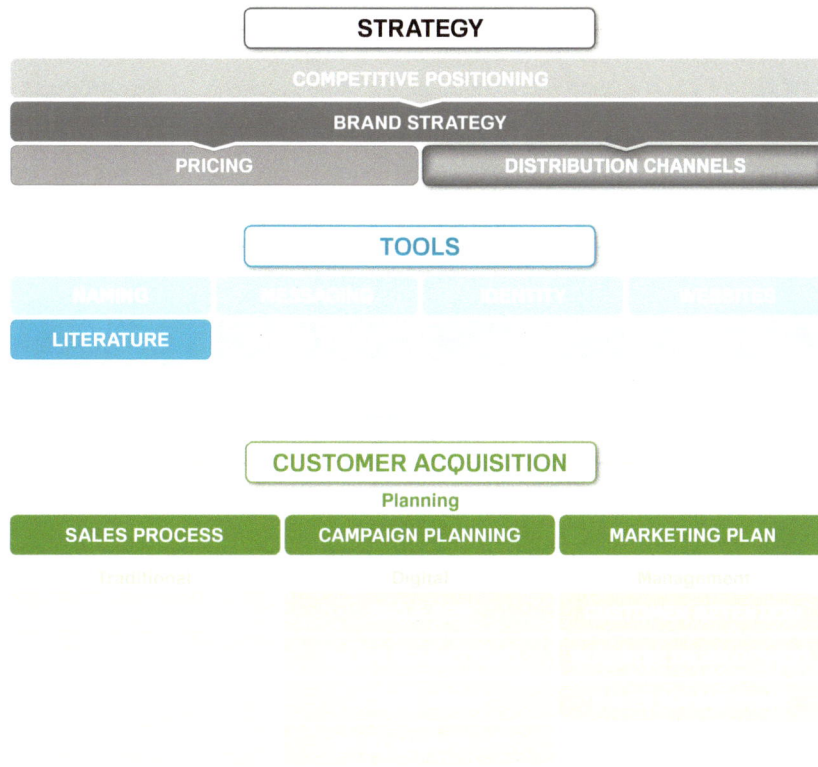

Distribution, also known as placement, is one of the classic "4 Ps" of marketing (product, promotion, price, placement). It's a key element of your strategy—it helps you expand your reach to penetrate your market.

B2B and B2C companies can sell through a single channel or through multiple channels that may include:

› **Direct/Internet:** Selling through your own e-commerce website.

› **Direct/Sales Team:** One or more sales teams that you employ directly. You may use multiple teams that specialize in different products or customer segments.

› **Direct/Catalog:** Selling through your own catalog.

› **Retail:** Retailers sell directly to end-users via a physical store, a website or a catalog.

› **Wholesaler/Distributor:** A company that buys products in bulk from many manufacturers and then resells smaller volumes to resellers or retailers.

› **Value-Added Reseller (VAR):** A VAR works with end-users to provide custom solutions that may include multiple products and services from different manufacturers.

› **Consultant:** A consultant develops relationships with companies and provides various types of services; they may recommend a manufacturer's product or simply purchase it to deliver a solution to their client.

› **Dealer:** A company or person who buys inventory from either a manufacturer or a distributor, then resells it to an end-user.

› **Sales Agent/Manufacturer's Rep:** You can outsource your sales function to a company that sells different manufacturers' products to a group of similar customers in a specific territory.

Here are three distribution examples:

Direct to End-Users	Sell Through a Dealer Network	Sell Through a VAR (Value-Added Reseller)
You have a sales team that sells directly to Fortune 100 companies. You have a second product line for small businesses. Instead of using your sales team, you sell this line directly to end-users through your website and marketing campaigns. You have two markets and two distribution channels.	You sell a product through a geographical network of dealers, who sell to end-users in their areas. The dealers may service the product as well. Your dealers are essentially your customers, and you have a strong program to train and support them with marketing campaigns and materials.	You sell a product to a company who bundles it with services or other products and resells it. That company is called a Value Added Reseller (VAR) because it adds value to your product. A VAR may work with an end-user to determine the right products and configurations, and then implement a system that includes your product.

To create a good distribution program, focus on the needs of your end-users.

> If users need personalized service, you can utilize a local dealer network or reseller program to provide that service.

> If your users prefer to buy online, you can create an e-commerce website and fulfillment system and sell direct; you can also sell to another online retailer or distributor that can offer your product on their own sites.

> You can build your own specialized sales team to prospect and close deals directly with customers.

Wholesalers, resellers, retailers, consultants and agents already have resources and relationships to quickly bring your product to market. If you sell through these groups instead of (or in addition to) selling direct, treat the entire channel as a group of customers—and they are, since they're buying your product and reselling it. Understand their needs and deliver strong marketing programs; you'll maximize everyone's revenue in the process.

Best Case	Neutral Case	Worst Case
You've used one or more distribution channels to grow your revenue and market share more quickly than you would have otherwise. Your end-users get the information and service they need before and after the sale. If you reach your end-user through wholesalers, VARs or other channel partners, you've created many successful marketing programs to drive revenue through your channel and you're committed to their success.	You're using one or more distribution channels with average success. You may not have as many channel partners as you'd like, but your current system is working moderately well. You devote resources to the program, but you wonder whether you'd be better off building an alternative distribution method—one that could help you grow more aggressively than you are growing now.	You probably aren't hitting your revenue goals because your distribution strategy is in trouble. With your current system, you may not be effectively reaching your end-users; your prospects probably aren't getting the information and service they need to buy your product. Your current system may also be difficult to manage. For example, channel members may not sell at your suggested price; they don't follow up on leads you deliver; they don't service the product very well and you're taking calls from angry customers.

SHARE
this ebook:

How Distribution Aligns with Strategy

Your distribution channels should support your positioning and brand strategy. These methods of reaching your market should be natural ways to access your market segments, and support the experience that your brand delivers.

For example, if you're selling a unique product that has little competition and is considered "high-end," you don't want to be carried in Walmart, where the majority of shoppers are looking for low-priced products that they're already familiar with.

Or, if you're an enterprise software vendor, you should be working with professional services firms who have deep experience with complex enterprise software deployments, and are a natural fit to engage with the types of companies that you target.

You can evaluate a new distribution channel or improve your channel marketing / management at any time. It's especially important to think about distribution when you're going after a new customer segment, releasing a new product, or looking for ways to aggressively grow your business.

Key Concepts & Steps

Evaluate how your end-users need to buy

Your distribution strategy should deliver the information and service your prospects need. For each customer segment, consider:

› How and where they prefer to buy
› Whether they need personalized education and training
› Whether they need additional products or services to be used along with yours
› Whether your product needs to be customized or installed
› Whether your product needs to be serviced

Match end-user needs to a distribution strategy

› If your end-users need a great deal of information and service, your company can deliver it directly through a sales force. You can also build a channel of qualified resellers or consultants. The size of the market and your price will probably dictate which scenario is best.
› If the buying process is fairly straightforward, you can sell direct via a website/catalog or perhaps through a wholesale/retail structure. You may also use an inbound telemarketing group or a field sales team.
› If you need complete control over your product's delivery and service, adding a channel partner probably isn't right for you.

Identify natural partners

If you want to grow beyond the direct model, look for companies that have relationships with your end-users. If consultants, wholesalers or retailers already reach your customer base, they're natural partners.

Build your channel

If you're setting up a distribution channel with one or more partners, treat it as a sales process:

› Approach the potential channel partner and "sell" the value of the partnership.
› Establish goals, service requirements and reporting requirements.
› Deliver inventory (if necessary) and sales/support materials.
› Train the partner.
› Run promotions and programs to support the partner and help them increase sales.

Minimize pricing conflicts

If you use multiple channels, carefully map out the price for each step in your channel, and include a fair profit for each type of partner. Then compare the price that the end-user will pay—if a customer can buy from one channel at a lower price than from another, your partners will rightfully have concerns. Pricing conflict is common, and it can jeopardize your entire strategy, so do your best to map out the price at each step and develop the best solution possible.

Drive revenue through the channel

Service your channel partners as you'd service your best customers and work with them to drive revenue. For example, provide them with marketing funds or materials to promote your products; run campaigns to generate leads and forward them to your partners.

Next Steps

If you're creating a new channel, you'll need a pricing strategy. You'll also need to deliver sales tools and literature, and a sales process.

When your channel is up and running, you can start launching marketing campaigns to channel partners and end-users, and manage the campaigns and partners throughout the year.

Naming

STRATEGY

COMPETITIVE POSITIONING

BRAND STRATEGY

TOOLS

| NAMING | MESSAGING | IDENTITY | WEBSITES |

| LITERATURE |

CUSTOMER ACQUISITION

Planning

CAMPAIGN PLANNING

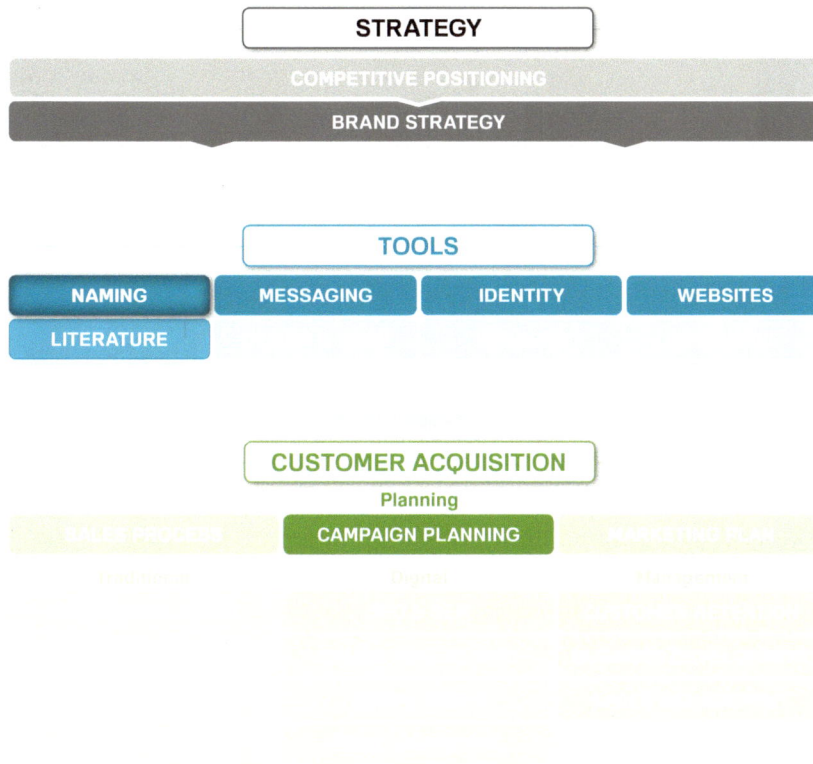

How important is the name of your product, service or company?

Your name is a critical extension of your brand, and it can reinforce the value you provide or distance you from it. When you're developing a name, you have a number of options:

› Use the founder or inventor's name (Hewlett-Packard)

› Describe what you do (Southwest Airlines)

› Describe an experience or image (Sprint)

› Take a word out of context (Apple)

› Make up a word (Google)

It's important to decide what your name should mean and represent. For example, if you're running a company that provides naming services, your name is a sample of your work—it should be great, right?

Here are some companies that provide naming services:

Unique	Average	Forgettable
These companies appear to be more creative and better at finding a name that stands out from the competition: › A Hundred Monkeys › Igor	These companies all sound the same: › The Naming Co. › Brighter Naming › Tradebrand › Catchword › Namebase › Lasting Names › Name One!	These naming agencies have forgettable names: › Werner & Stevens › Wollenski Associates *(While they are hypothetical examples, there are a lot of naming companies named after their founders!)*

All of these companies may provide great services, have many years of experience, and have terrific track records. If you needed to select three companies to bid on your naming project, which companies would you contact? Are you more likely to call a company with a unique name, an average name, or a forgettable name?

This example reinforces that you have one chance to make a first impression. Many of your potential customers might know virtually nothing about your company, product or service, and a great name can make a positive impression and open doors. A weak name can close them.

The name selection process is especially challenging because there are more than 26 million businesses in the United States. U.S. trademark law protects business names, so when you find one you like, make sure you can use it. If you infringe on a trademark, you could be forced to abandon your new name after investing a lot of time and money in it.

Also think about your internet marketing goals, since you may have to find a URL to match your name. There are almost 200 million domain names registered worldwide, and some experts believe that over 98% of words in the dictionary are registered as domain names.

Don't let these challenges stop you from finding the best name you can—there's a lot at stake.

Best Case	Neutral Case	Worst Case
A great name can create buzz, position you as a true leader and innovator, and reinforce your positioning and brand in a word or two. That's powerful. It can convey a culture, a position, and differentiate the company from the rest of the market.	You look and sound like everybody else. You've missed an opportunity to convey an important message, but at least you're not hurting yourself.	A poor name can neutralize or even negate the work you do to build a position in the market. You may have trouble generating interest in your company, product or service, forcing you to spend more time and money educating the market about your value. A poor name can also limit your opportunities if you expand into other markets.

How Naming Aligns with Strategy

Your company name is the anchor for your brand strategy—typically the first thing that the market sees and hears.

Your name, logo, packaging (colors, fonts, and design), location (if the market visits your store or offices), tagline or slogan, and unique ownable specialty (your mindshare) all work in concert to create a perception.

When launching a new consumer product, seasoned marketers often create their positioning, brand, distribution and pricing strategies before they select a product name, to ensure that all are aligned at launch. With tens of millions of dollars at stake, it's important to get it right the first time.

Most small-to-midsize companies select a name to open their business, then build their brand, distribution and pricing over time. That's fine, but it's important to work to align them, to give you the best chance at delivering a repeatable brand experience and owning a unique perception in the mind of the market.

Key Concepts & Steps

Do you need to hire a consultant or agency to help with your name?

With a good process and strategy, you can probably develop a good name on your own. However, you may not have the resources or desire to handle the project internally. While it's no guarantee that a firm or consultant will develop a better name, they may do it more quickly and objectively.

There are a number of factors to consider, including:

› The stakes—if you're investing a lot of money into launching a new product to a major market with established competition, the stakes are high.
› Your confidence in your team's creative firepower or objectivity.
› The amount of time and energy you have to devote to the project.
› Whether you can afford to bring in an outside resource.

Develop a strategy

› Determine what your name needs to accomplish.
› Decide how it will work with existing product or service names (if applicable).
› Determine what kind of name to develop—descriptive, invented, founder's name, etc.
› Develop objective criteria to evaluate the names you generate.

Generate plenty of potential names

If you're competing beyond your local area, you may find that many of your potential names (or URLs) are already taken, so you'll need to create a long list. Invite a variety of people to a brainstorming session. Plan it well and capture every idea for further evaluation.

Evaluate the list against your criteria

Your goal is to objectively find the name that meets your criteria, so be careful about asking friends and family whether they "like" a name. For example, a name that raises eyebrows may do so because it's different—and it may be the most memorable and powerful one in the bunch.

Also test the name to make sure it:

› Sounds good over the phone

› Won't be constantly mispronounced or misspelled, which defeats the purpose of a name

› Isn't confusing

› Conveys what you need it to convey

› Has a URL that works with it

Protect your name

It's important to protect your name to the appropriate degree. If you choose a name that infringes on another company's trademark, you could receive a cease-and-desist letter and have to go to court and/or change your name after months or even years of use.

By protecting your name, you also gain the ability to prevent future competitors from using it.

Next Steps

After you select a new name, you can create your logo and corporate identity, and then begin creating the messages to use throughout your sales tools and literature, and your campaign creative.

Messaging

STRATEGY		
COMPETITIVE POSITIONING		
BRAND STRATEGY		

TOOLS		
NAMING	MESSAGING	WEBSITES
LITERATURE		

CUSTOMER ACQUISITION

Planning

CAMPAIGN PLANNING

Traditional	Digital
TRADITIONAL MEDIA	SEO & SEM
DIRECT MAIL	ONLINE ADVERTISING
PUBLICITY	SOCIAL MEDIA
TELEMARKETING	EMAIL MARKETING
EVENTS	

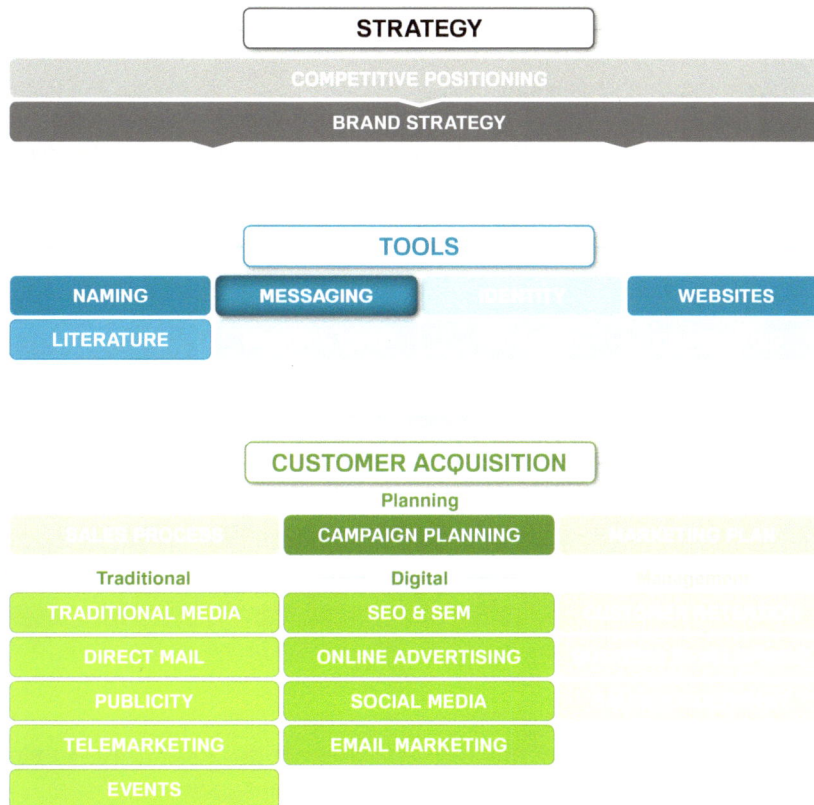

How do you respond when someone asks "what does your company/product/service do?" Do all your team members answer the same way? Is your response compelling enough to make the listener want to learn more, or do you sound like everyone else?

"Messages" are written and verbal statements that quickly describe what you do and how you're different. They're used throughout your interactions with your market such as:

› The "elevator pitch"—the 30-second response to "what do you do?"

› Sales and marketing materials—sales literature, websites, presentations and campaigns

› The introductory statement in a phone call

› Press releases—the blurb at the bottom of the release that explains what the company does

› Slogans

› Your mission statement

Good messages emphasize and support your positioning and brand strategy. They hone in on what's important to your market and communicate it consistently and effectively.

DOWNLOAD hundreds of plans for these marketing activities at www.MarketingMO.com.

marketing MO

SHARE this ebook:

19

Best Case	Neutral Case	Worst Case
By carefully crafting your messages, you can strengthen your positioning, your brand and the reasons your markets should buy from you. It's easy to communicate your value. The market "gets it" very quickly, speeding up the sales process.	Ho-hum messages don't help you stand out, but as long as they're not inaccurate or poorly written, they probably won't hurt. You are missing out on the opportunity to strengthen your position.	Without a set of documented messages, individual team members do their own authoring. The results are inconsistent and rarely good. Weak and inconsistent messages confuse the market and can contradict the other strategies you've worked hard to implement.

How Messaging Aligns with Strategy

Consistent messaging is essential to communicating the ideas and concepts of your competitive positioning and brand strategy to your market. It allows you to effectively communicate what you stand for and the value that your offering provides.

Your messages should have a personality, a tone, and a purpose, and should align with the elements of your brand to be most effective.

Key Concepts & Steps

Define your writing style and requirements

Before you start writing, define your style requirements—tone, voice, style, vocabulary—to ensure the writing will be consistent and match your brand strategy.

Create an elevator pitch

The elevator pitch describes who you are, what you do, who your customers are and why they should buy from you. After you've written it, read it out loud to see how it sounds and how long it takes (no more than 30 seconds).

Create your positioning statements

Write statements of various lengths—25, 50 and 100 words—so you have a message length that fits a variety of materials. The shorter statements focus on the value and positioning; the longer statements also include features and benefits.

Create a tagline/slogan

Your tagline/slogan is a more succinct phrase used in campaigns. It can be a few words or a short phrase—and for most business writers, it's harder to create. You may want to hire a copywriter for this one.

Create your mission statement

An average mission statement describes why you're in business. A great mission statement is compelling, shows why you're different and conveys your company's personality.

Determine where to use the messages

Make sure to use your new messages consistently. Train your team to use the messages and audit your materials periodically to make sure they're still working in the future.

Next Steps

Your messages feed all of your communication with your market. Use them in your sales tools and literature, your website and in your marketing campaigns.

Corporate Identity

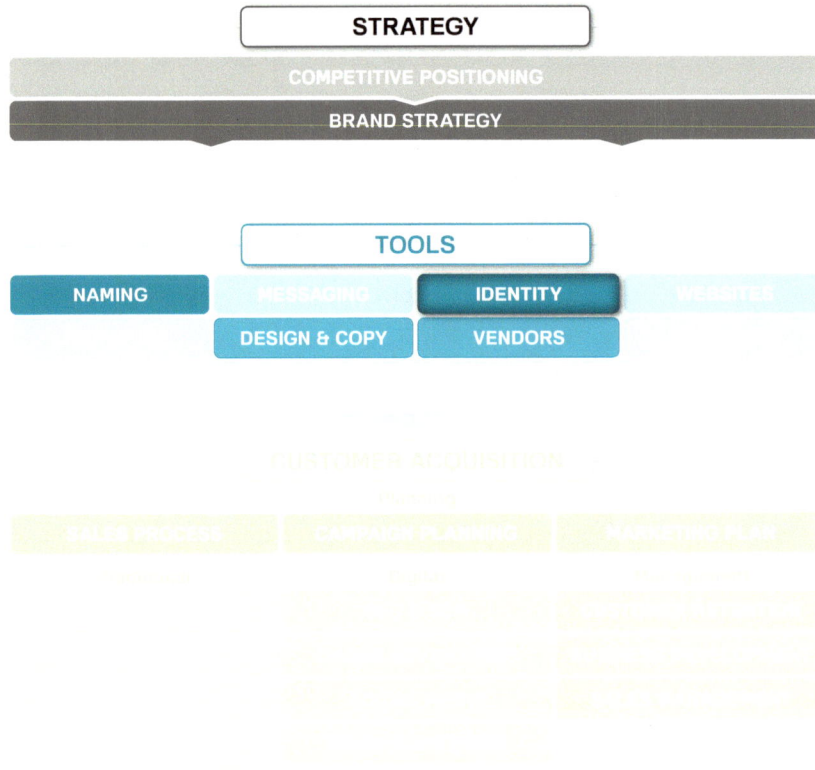

STRATEGY

COMPETITIVE POSITIONING

BRAND STRATEGY

TOOLS

NAMING	MESSAGING	IDENTITY	WEBSITES
	DESIGN & COPY	VENDORS	

When was the last time someone gave you a fantastic business card? Did you turn it over and look at it closely? Did you comment on it? And did you generate some sort of impression of that person and company?

Corporate identity is an extension of your brand and includes everything that has your logo or contact information on it:

> Business cards

> Envelopes

> Letterhead

> Mailing labels

> Email templates & signatures

> Fax covers

> Proposal/quote templates

> Invoices/statements

> Memos

> Signage

> Promotional items

Many companies spend time and money on things like business cards yet overlook proposal templates, invoices and email signatures—items that your prospects and customers see more frequently. When an employee customizes an email template with unusual designs or fonts, it can contradict an expensive and serious business card—and convey a far different impression to the customer.

Each element in your identity should use the same fonts, colors, and layout. The design itself may not be incredibly important unless you're in a creative field, but consistency and professionalism make an impression. In many cases it may be a first impression, so why not make a good one?

Best Case	Neutral Case	Worst Case
Every touch with your prospects and customers is consistent and professional. They see a simple, effective design that conveys your brand and delivers a consistent experience.	Some of your identity is great and other things, like invoices or shipping labels, don't match up. Prospects and customers probably notice, but you don't think it's a problem.	Your prospects and customers see a mishmash of poorly-produced identity. They may wonder how you can deliver the product or service you're selling if you can't produce a professional-looking document.

How Corporate Identity Aligns with Strategy

Your corporate identity represents your company brand. It should support the visual brand requirements of your brand strategy, and be consistent throughout all of your print and digital materials.

Key Concepts & Steps

Evaluate your current identity usage

If you're already in business, does all of your identity reflect your brand?

Check everything from invoices and shipping labels to email signatures. Make sure that your logo is used correctly (sometimes they get re-sized) and that all of your materials are consistent with your positioning and brand strategy. For example, if you're focusing on innovative, expensive new products but you have flimsy business cards, you're not reinforcing your brand.

Create professional, consistent templates for every touch point with your market

Use a consistent style for everything your company sends out. It may take only ten minutes to create a better template, and that template may be seen by hundreds or thousands of prospects and customers over time.

Keep inventory

Templates can be altered or misplaced. Make sure that your team knows how to use them and check them regularly.

Next Steps

Once you've finished evaluating your identity, the typical next step is to focus on your sales tools and literature, as well as your website.

Websites

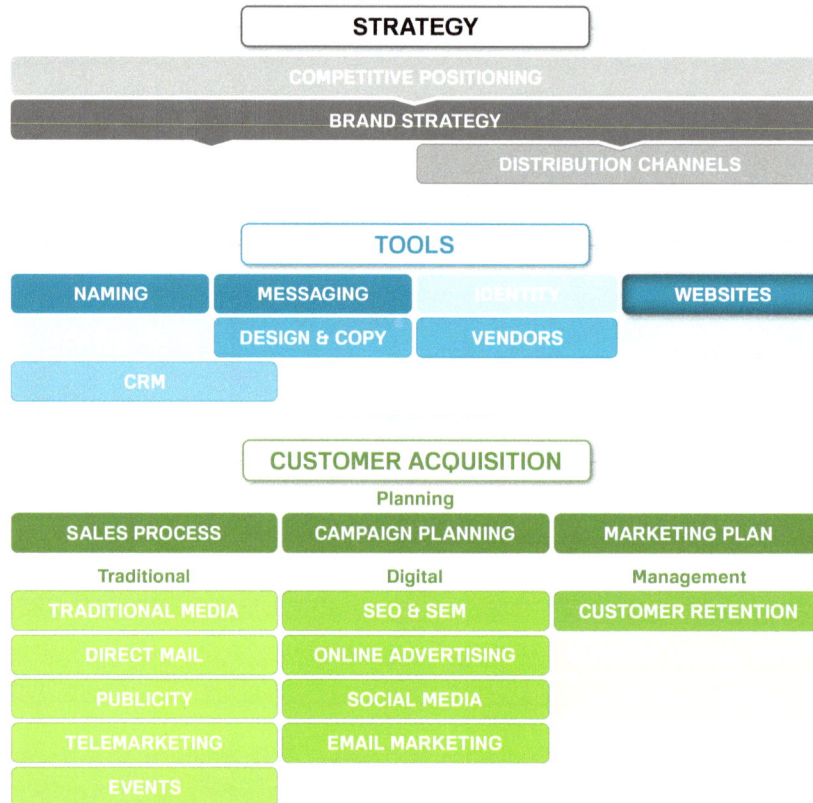

Your website is potentially the most powerful sales and marketing tool in your arsenal.

A good site plays an enormous role in your sales process and can help you to reinforce your brand, generate leads and support customers. Think of your site as your storefront that serves different groups and converts visitors into prospects and customers. It can help you:

› Generate leads

› Nurture existing leads and move them closer to purchase

› Build brand awareness

› Deliver information about your products and services in a compelling way

› Process orders, cross- and up-sell, and run special promotions

› Communicate with existing customers and distribution channels

› Communicate with partners, investors and potential new employees

› Generate publicity

Although a good website can be a substantial investment, it doesn't have to be expensive. It just needs to effectively communicate with your market and support your brand. When you develop your site with rich content and some basic marketing functionality, you gain broad and potentially lucrative marketing capabilities.

SHARE
this ebook:

Best Case	Neutral Case	Worst Case
Your site is more than a brochure—it sells. You use it for a variety of internet marketing campaigns: search, social, email, webinars, ongoing communications, publicity and more. Your content is relevant; you know how many leads your campaigns generate and what those leads cost. You can quickly create landing pages for campaigns so you can convert traffic into prospects.	You have a standard site with basic information plus a few press releases and newsletters. You've tried some internet marketing with mixed results. You know your prospects look at your site and it could be better, but it's no different than your competitors. There are bigger priorities than a site redesign, but you suspect that more content and functionality would give you more marketing power.	Your site works against you. It may be the design, content (or lack of), writing, or functionality. It doesn't support your positioning and you can't use it any internet marketing campaigns. You wince when prospects ask for the URL; you know that they don't get a good impression from your site and your competitors look better and stronger. You can't quantify whether you've lost any business—but you know that you probably have.

How Websites Align with Strategy

Before building (or redesigning) a website, make sure that you've reviewed your competitive positioning and brand strategy. Your website should support them. The copy on your website should reflect the consistent messages that you've developed.

For many businesses, their website is their most important marketing tool—it is often a customer's first experience with the brand. Your website may also play an integral role in your sales process and customer retention programs.

Key Concepts & Steps

Develop your project team and timeline
› Work backwards from key deadlines to create your project timeline. Give yourself plenty of leeway since website projects can easily hit snags.
› If you're launching a sophisticated site, make sure you've included all of the relevant departments in your project team.

Define your needs
Before you hire a designer or developer, decide what your site needs to accomplish:
› Your major goals.
› How the site will support online and traditional marketing campaigns.
› How the site will help you generate leads, nurture prospects, communicate with your market, process orders and provide customer service.
› The information and functionality you believe you'll need.
› Whether a basic design is fine or whether you'll need something more unique and customized.

Develop your content

› Determine a preliminary game plan for your internet marketing efforts so that your site can support them.

› List the "users" who will visit your site: new prospects, existing prospects, customers, partners, media, job applicants, vendors, etc.

› Develop a list of the information and tools ("content") that each user wants to find on your site.

› Review competitor and industry sites for additional ideas.

Organize the content

Organize your content so users can quickly find what they need. You'll also need to incorporate search engine optimization (SEO) techniques to help with search engine rankings. For example, your home page is most important to search engines; if you don't get that page optimized for specific keywords, you won't rank as highly.

Identify the functionality you'll need

Different types of functionality often require different programming solutions.

› Determine whether you want to allow customers to do things like view product details, process orders, and access their records on the site.

› Evaluate other functionality such as support forums, search, calculators, streaming video, etc.

› Determine the type of content management system you need to support your SEO and SEM needs.

Develop your design requirements

Like your sales literature, your site should support your brand. Use your regular color palette, typefaces and personality traits as much as possible.

Identify any last requirements

› Requirements for updating and managing the content

› Programming technologies you do and don't want in the site

› Reporting requirements

Qualify and hire vendors

Unless you have an in-house web development team, hire vendor(s) for design, programming, copywriting and/or SEO. Review their past work and talk with recent clients to make sure that you're comfortable with their strategy and skills.

Next Steps

Once you've finished your site, use it in your marketing campaigns to communicate with your market.

Sales Tools & Literature

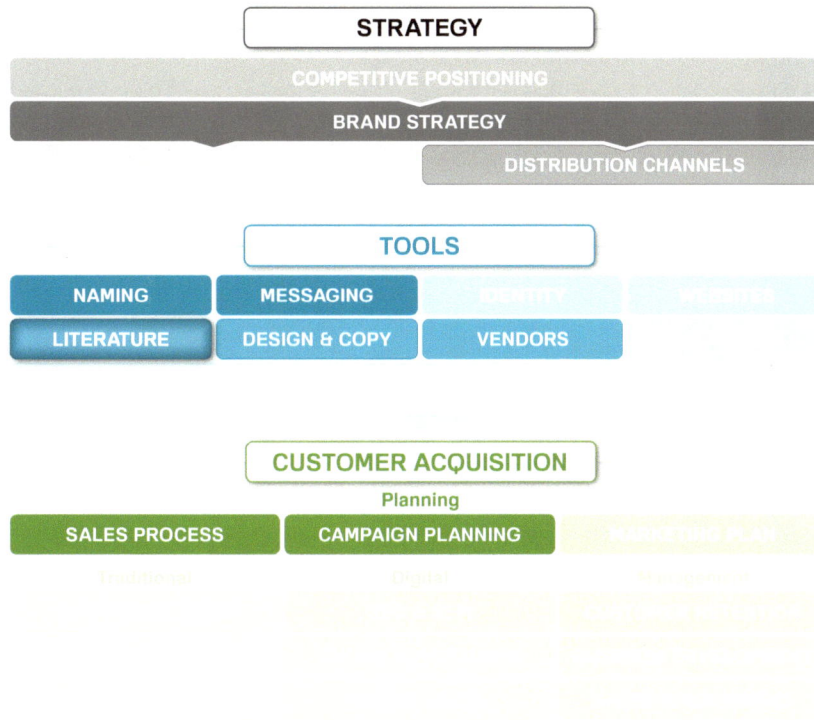

Do you know many B2B companies that can sell their product or service without literature or other supporting materials?

Sales tools and literature help you communicate and strengthen your messages. They're also known as "marketing communications" or "collateral" and may include:

- Brochures
- Product data sheets
- Case studies
- White papers
- PowerPoint presentations
- Websites
- Newsletters
- Reference lists
- Proposal templates
- Calculators

The printed word carries a lot of credibility, so your materials are important tools in your arsenal. They reinforce your brand and can create a lasting impression on your prospects. A single printed or digital piece can reach multiple decision makers when your primary contact passes it along, and can even go viral if distributed on the web.

Sales tools and literature are more common in B2B than B2C (which relies more on marketing campaign messages and branding) but many B2C companies use sales tools and literature to promote their offerings to wholesalers, distributors and retailers.

Good literature and tools should be tightly integrated into your sales process. Rather than inundating a prospect with all of your information at once, break out the information into distinct pieces that answer a prospect's key questions at a specific stage in the process. As a result, your prospects can quickly absorb what's most relevant, make decisions quickly and move to the next stage.

Best Case	Neutral Case	Worst Case
Your sales literature and tools are strong components of your marketing arsenal. They convey your brand, speak directly to your market, and deliver the right amount of information at the right time. They truly help you move prospects through the sales process as quickly as possible.	Your literature and tools are typical and general. They convey much of the information your prospects need, but lack the singular focus to be as effective as they could be.	Your literature and tools don't support your brand and positioning—they're working against you. You haven't defined your typical selling process for moving prospects through the buying process, and haven't created sales tools to address the typical questions buyers have as they evaluate your product or service.

How Sales Tools and Literature Align with Strategy

Your sales tools and literature should support your positioning, brand strategy and messaging. They're used to drill down into more specific areas of your offering.

Key Concepts & Steps

Analyze your current materials

If you feel that your existing literature and tools could be more effective, take inventory:

› Review each piece to determine its sole focus.

› Ask your sales team and others for feedback on whether the piece is effective.

› Make sure that the piece supports your positioning and brand strategy.

› Make sure that each piece is delivered at the right time.

Determine what materials you need

List the steps of your sales process, then:

› Brainstorm about the materials you could use to answer a prospect's questions at each step.

› Define a singular purpose for each piece of literature or tool.

Write, design & print your materials

To develop your content, focus on the singular purpose of each piece.

› Outline the content that should be included in each piece.

› Hire vendors for design and writing if needed.

› Research and write the content.

› Develop your design requirements.

› Design the piece.

› Get quotes and work with your chosen printer to ensure that you're happy with the final outcome.

Train your team to use the materials

Make sure that everyone understands the purpose of each piece and when to use it.

Next Steps

Determine where and how to use your sales tools and literature—on your website, with your sales team, and in your marketing campaigns.

Your sales tools should align with your sales process, to provide the granular details that prospects need as they move through the steps of their buying decision.

Copywriting & Graphic Design

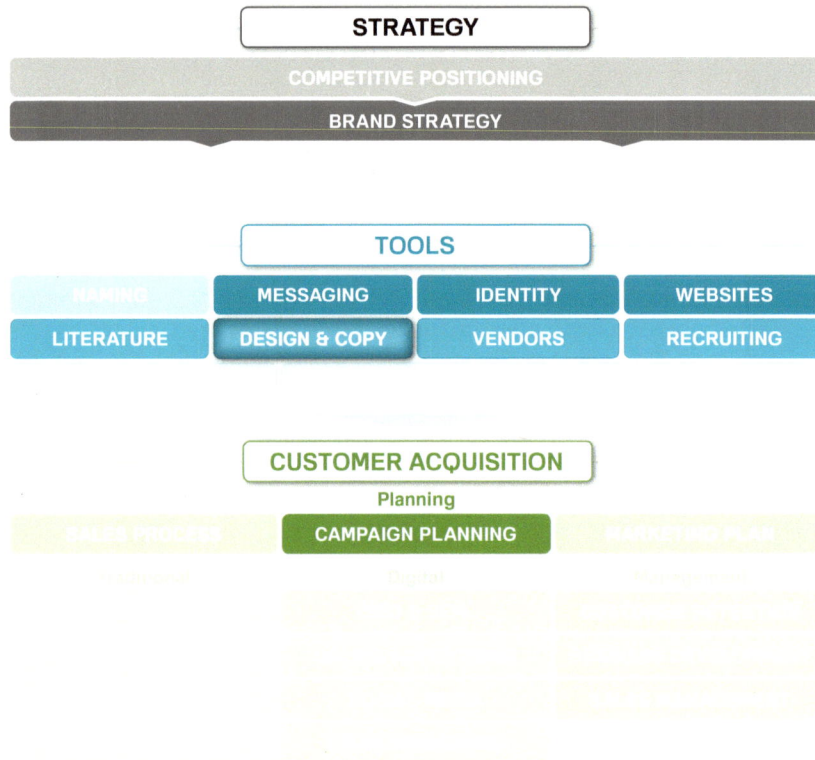

STRATEGY
COMPETITIVE POSITIONING
BRAND STRATEGY

TOOLS		
NAMING	MESSAGING	IDENTITY	WEBSITES
LITERATURE	DESIGN & COPY	VENDORS	RECRUITING

CUSTOMER ACQUISITION
Planning
CAMPAIGN PLANNING

Design and copy are essential tools for any brand. They play a major role in supporting positioning and shaping a brand experience.

Brands are built by what we see, hear and touch. Our sensory experiences work together to create feelings and emotions, which create perceptions. These perceptions sometimes capture a piece of our mind—when we decide what something is "known for."

Think about the elements of your brand that are defined by copywriting and graphic design:

› Logos and corporate identity
› Product packaging
› Websites
› Interior and exterior signs
› Campaign messages and creative (delivered via websites, search engines, social media sites, print publications, radio, television, email, direct mail, and in-person via events, store displays, telemarketing and sales)

These account for a substantial part of most brands' experience—everything but the people who represent your brand, your product or service itself, your physical locations, and music or audio that you use.

Most companies use an array of copywriters and designers throughout the year. Since writers and designers typically have strengths in specific areas, the challenge is to find the resources for the right projects.

SHARE
this ebook:

For example, copywriters can specialize in ad print ad copy, website copy, TV and radio copy, articles and blog posts, press releases, creative storytelling, white papers and brochures, presentation writing, technical writing, or persuasive sales copy.

Designers often specialize in logos and corporate identity, digital design for websites, print ad design, print brochure design, digital presentation design, illustration, photography selection, or interactive design.

A great web designer might produce mediocre print ads; a great ad copywriter might produce thin website copy.

The key to maximizing the effectiveness of your copy and design is to understand what types of skills you need for different projects, and have access to a talent pool (or be able to find the right talent for the job). Once you have the right resource in place, a well-written creative brief (which includes detailed brand guidelines) should give your creative resource the understanding they need to do their job.

Best Case	Neutral Case	Worst Case
Your copy and design are powerful; they communicate your objectives simply, in a memorable way and are consistent across all mediums. This doesn't mean that all the copy is the same; it simply means that the design and copy consistently work together to convey your personality and create a consistent experience. Your market "gets it" quickly . . . and you leave a lasting impression.	Your copy and design aren't bad—some is really effective and some isn't. You realize that your team has strengths and weaknesses, but you don't have alternative options so you make do with what you have. You know that you could create a more consistent and effective experience, but you don't feel that it's hurting you too much.	Naturally, the worst case scenario is that your copy is poorly written, and your design unappealing. Your materials are inconsistent, and often create a negative impression with your market. You have scant copywriting and design resources, either due to lack of budget, or an inability to find the right resources for the right project. Your competitors' brands are stronger, and you feel that you're losing market share because of it.

How Copywriting and Graphic Design Align with Strategy

It's difficult to build a strong brand without effective and consistent copy and design. They play a major role in shaping your brand, affecting most of the touchpoints with your market.

They're a critical tool for executing your positioning and brand strategy—they're a key part of your tactics—this is where you "do things right."

Key Concepts & Steps

Identify the strengths of your resources

Review the skills of your in-house team and pool of contractors and create a list or database that identifies who excels at specific types of work.

Create a project timeline for each marketing piece

Provide a reasonable amount of time between each step so each team member can deliver on schedule. The earlier you get started, the better your results.

Determine what content will be in the piece

Content should drive the design, not the reverse. If you start with design and try to fill in content later, the piece may not be nearly as effective. Identify the copy, graphics, photos or charts that you'll need in your piece before starting the design process.

Use a creative brief

A creative brief is an overview for a project. It can be simple or lengthy, depending on the complexity of the project and the amount of background information your team needs. A good creative brief defines:

> Deadlines

> Goals, including the action you want the recipients to take after seeing the piece

> Audience

> Content

> Background information about the product, service, audience, company, etc.

> Branding requirements including the desired color palette, logo usage, fonts, voice, tone and personality to convey

Establish criteria for the designs

It's much easier to evaluate design concepts when you have specific criteria to measure against. Establish those criteria upfront so your design team understands what they need to deliver, and then use them to choose concepts and provide feedback.

Pay attention to proofs and the press check

Make sure that you have a very thorough review process in place—a typo in an ad or brochure can be an expensive and embarrassing error. And conduct a thorough press check so your printed materials completely match your requirements and vision; you wouldn't want your brochure printed on the wrong paper or your colors to be mismatched.

Next Steps

Keep looking for good copywriters and graphic designers with strengths in different areas.

With a good team of resources, you'll have someone to call on, no matter what type of campaign idea or tool you dream up.

SHARE
this ebook:

Vendor Selection

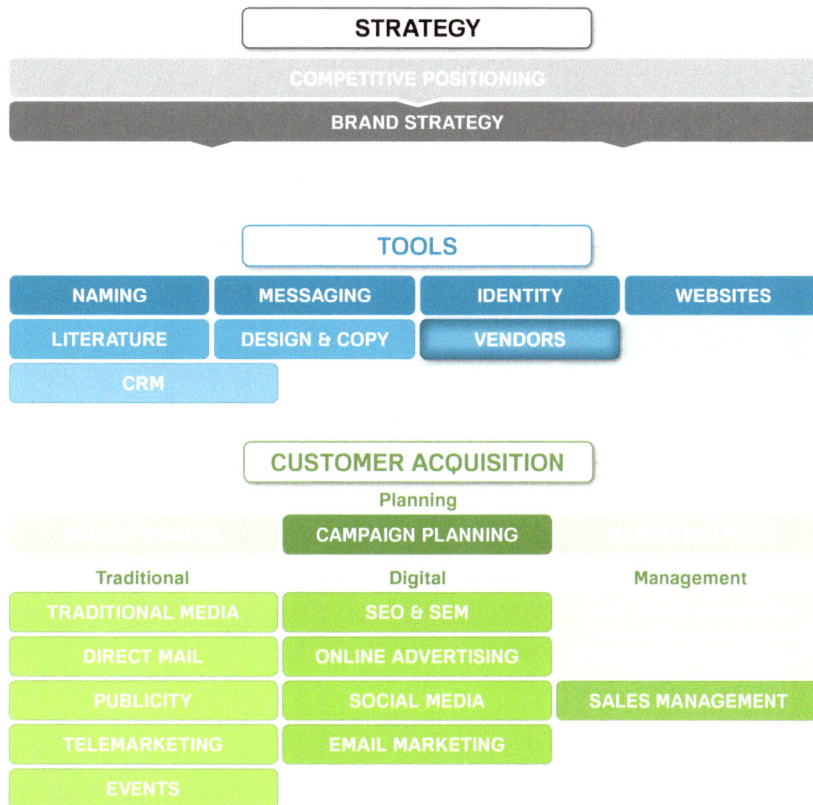

STRATEGY			
COMPETITIVE POSITIONING			
BRAND STRATEGY			

TOOLS

NAMING	MESSAGING	IDENTITY	WEBSITES
LITERATURE	DESIGN & COPY	VENDORS	
CRM			

CUSTOMER ACQUISITION

Planning

CAMPAIGN PLANNING

Traditional	Digital	Management
TRADITIONAL MEDIA	SEO & SEM	
DIRECT MAIL	ONLINE ADVERTISING	
PUBLICITY	SOCIAL MEDIA	SALES MANAGEMENT
TELEMARKETING	EMAIL MARKETING	
EVENTS		

Vendors play a key role in most company's marketing activities. The explosive growth of the Internet has fundamentally changed the marketing function, giving marketers a tremendous amount of new avenues to use for connecting with their audiences.

The downside for marketers is the challenge of choosing which new digital mediums to use, and executing the tactics in these new areas.

Some marketing leaders have decided to focus their departments on designing strategies and carefully managing outsourced vendors that handle execution. Outsourcing allows marketers to gain deep expertise across a number of different areas, providing better results at a lower cost than if they hired the talent for in-house execution.

For example, a seasoned marketing director and a team of a few marketing managers and coordinators could leverage vendors to:

› Build and execute digital marketing campaigns, including social media campaigns, online advertising, and SEO and SEM

› Design and build websites, microsites and mobile apps

› Purchase traditional media in print, radio and television

› Write persuasive copy for sales tools and presentations

› Design brand elements, including logos and corporate identity

› Generate online and offline publicity

› Create print collateral, including brochures, data sheets, posters and signage

› Use telemarketing to reach their audience

- Create product packaging and displays
- Design and fulfill direct mail campaigns
- Manage events

The most successful marketing departments using this "outsourced" model understand what types of vendors they need to execute their strategy, have a well-defined vetting and vendor selection process, and carefully manage vendor deliverables, timeframes and costs.

Do you see your company in any of these scenarios?

Best Case	Neutral Case	Worst Case
You have a clear understanding of the specific types of vendors that you need, and have either a pool of well-qualified vendors to choose from, or understand how to select and manage a new vendor. Your team requires vendors to adhere to strict project scopes, deadlines and costs, and you always have a clear understanding of a vendor's performance. As a result, your vendors consistently deliver great results that are on time and on budget. This gives you time to focus on developing strategies and measuring results. Your vendors truly enhance your business.	You use some vendors for specific activities. Some perform well, and others don't, extending deadlines, producing mediocre work and going over budget. After handing off a project, you check in occasionally to see how the vendor is progressing, but as the deadline nears, you're a bit nervous—hoping for good results. Often times you get them, but it doesn't surprise you when you don't. If you had more reliable vendors, you'd be able to contribute more efforts to measuring and improving campaign performance, and designing new strategies to enhance your positioning and build your brand.	You rarely use vendors, trying to get as much done in-house as possible, but you wish you could outsource more to increase your bandwidth, and get better results. When you do outsource a project, it's a crapshoot whether you're going to get what you expect. You wish that your team did a better job managing vendors' progress, or at the minimum, could get the vendors to deliver decent work on time. You shy away from using new vendors, because you never know what you're going to get, and when you spend precious budget and receive poor results, you end up looking bad to your executive team.

How Vendor Selection Aligns with Strategy

Some vendors can be very helpful creating strategies in their areas of expertise, but others might develop strategies to promote the service that they're selling (i.e. to win or expand the engagement), so it's important to have a strong understanding of your goals before engaging a vendor on a big project.

Additionally, most vendors' work directly represents your brand, so make sure that these vendors have a strong understanding of your positioning and brand strategy, and ask them to show how their work supports it.

Key Concepts & Steps

Define your needs and timeline

Determine exactly what you're looking for before you start your vendor search. You may want to set an initial budget, and then develop a timeline for your search, especially if you have important deadlines to meet. If you don't address this beforehand, certain vendors may drive this process, adhering to a schedule that fits them, instead of what fits you.

Identify and analyze vendors

Use the Web and ask for referrals to find a list of qualified vendors. Develop a list of qualifying questions and narrow the field to a handful of companies.

Create your RFP

If you're looking for very simple, straightforward services, you can ask bidders to provide a proposal and quote. For more complex or intangible projects, it's better to create a Request for Proposal (RFP) that asks bidders to respond to very specific questions in a consistent fashion. A standard RFP is especially helpful when:

› The vendor is providing a comprehensive service

› The project is intangible or has many elements, such as a website

› You have very specific evaluation criteria and need to compare "apples to apples"

› You're evaluating a large number of bidders (more than four)

Then, evaluate, negotiate and award the project:

› Rate your bidders on the important criteria and narrow the field.

› Negotiate pricing and terms with your finalists, but remember the adage "You get what you pay for." Don't just choose the lowest bid—choose the vendor that best meets your criteria for success and fits within your budget.

Next Steps

Continue to improve your vendor research, RFPs, and vendor management. If you rely on vendors for collateral and customer acquisition activities, treat them as key members of your team. Good vendor selection and management will help you improve results.

STRATEGY

COMPETITIVE POSITIONING

BRAND STRATEGY

TOOLS

NAMING · MESSAGING · IDENTITY · WEBSITES

RECRUITING

CUSTOMER ACQUISITION

Planning

CAMPAIGN PLANNING | MARKETING PLAN

Management

CUSTOMER RETENTION

BUSINESS DEVELOPMENT

SALES MANAGEMENT

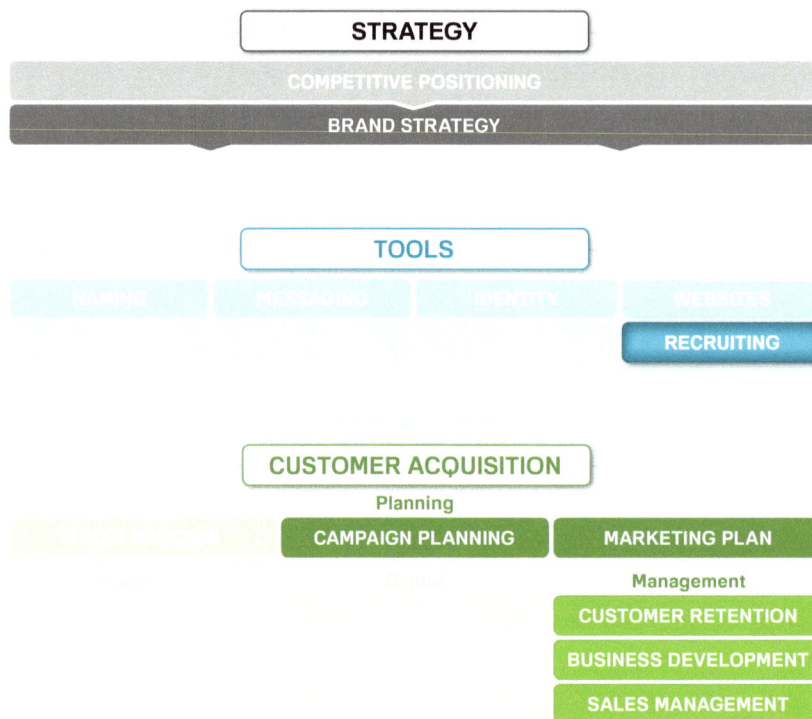

Many CEOs have gone on record saying "Our people are our greatest asset."

For many companies, their people heavily influence their brand. Think of a service company—the people delivering the service have the most interaction with the marketplace, and sometimes define the entire brand experience.

In some product companies and in most B2B companies, the sales and customer service teams play a heavy role in a customer's experience with the company.

The simplest way to build your team, department or company with good people who will represent your brand is to have a well-defined recruiting program.

Like marketing, recruiting is both an art and a science:

› **Art**: Getting to know a candidate to understand whether s/he is the best fit for the job.
› **Science**: Defining detailed job requirements so you can search for the right candidates; conducting a wide search; using a process for evaluating candidates; and measuring results.

Marketing leaders need to recruit talented people to help them turn their strategies into reality—coordinators, designers, managers, account reps, sales reps, telemarketers, and business development reps.

If you're a marketing leader, you might not currently influence hiring decisions with the sales team or in other areas of the company. While you don't have to become a human resources expert, if people in ANY area of your company represent your brand, it's a good idea to have your hiring teams evaluate your market-facing candidates against your brand personality traits.

When your company hires people that naturally represent your brand, it's a lot easier to deliver a consistent brand experience in the marketplace.

And when you use a standardized recruiting process for people involved in marketing and sales, you should end up with more consistent results.

Do you see your company in any of these scenarios?

Best Case	Neutral Case	Worst Case
Every market-facing employee understands your brand personality traits and the experience that you want to deliver. You have a strong marketing and sales team with the right skill sets to build the marketing tools and execute the customer acquisition activities that support your strategy.	Some of your market-facing employees represent your brand well, but others don't. The people in charge of your hiring have your brand guidelines, but you're not sure whether they're adhered to—you control the hires on your team, but not in other departments, including sales.	You haven't outlined your brand personality traits, but if you did, you're sure that not all of your market-facing employees would fit them. There are simply too many different types of personalities. And if you did define your brand and share it with your executive team, you're not sure whether they'd even buy into it.
Before each hire, you develop a solid job description, compensation plan and job profile so you're sure about the qualifications and personality type you need for the position.	You create job descriptions before you recruit and you usually receive an acceptable number of résumés.	You have some team members who aren't qualified for their roles. They require a great deal of management and you're concerned about the time that it'll take to replace them.
You screen and interview your candidates efficiently and when you hire someone, s/he's excited about the job. You have little turnover and your employees are truly a valuable asset to the company.	Sometimes the process drags out longer than it should, and you've hired some candidates that weren't a great fit. You do have some average performers on your team, but there are no major issues.	It's difficult to find qualified candidates, especially because experience is expensive. Morale isn't great and people view their job as tedious—there isn't a lot of excitement and positive energy in your team.

How Recruiting Aligns with Strategy

Every market-facing employee contributes to your brand experience, so getting the right people aboard directly affects the execution of your brand strategy.

You need talented people in your department to help you shape your strategies and manage execution, so good recruiting practices are an essential element in any high-performing marketing department.

And, if your positioning is clear and your brand is strong, candidates that support what you stand for will come to you; recruiting for a strong, well-defined brand is far easier than recruiting for an unknown, or poorly-defined brand.

Key Concepts & Steps

Share your brand guidelines with your entire leadership team

› Have all of the people in your company understand your brand's personality traits, and the experience that you wish to deliver.

› Use these during your screening and interviewing process. If people don't fit them, don't hire them.

› Incent your people to refer potential new employees who fit your criteria.

Define the position

› Evaluate the job responsibilities and prioritize the skills and experience that your candidates will need.

› Develop specific criteria you'll use to evaluate your candidates.

Write a compelling ad

› A good ad inspires qualified candidates to apply for the position. It needs to stand out among the ads they'll be reviewing, and it needs to convey credibility, your brand and your personality.

› Think of your ad as a sales pitch to a prospect and write it carefully.

Cast a wide net

› Referrals are a great source for qualified candidates. Encourage everyone in your company to contact vendors, customers, friends and family about open positions. Create a job description that they can pass around.

› Advertise in appropriate publications and websites. If you're concerned about cost, measure your cost per applicant and per hire, and then use the best-performing sources the next time around.

› If you're not finding qualified candidates, keep investing . . . don't settle for mediocre applicants just because you don't want to spend more money looking.

› If you're doing a lot of hiring, make sure to post open jobs on your website and include content that speaks to applicants. Good candidates will look at your site to learn about the company.

Follow your process

› Create a process and follow it: résumé review, phone screen, interview, second interview, reference check, and offer. A good process saves time—for example, don't invite a candidate for live interviews if you haven't completed a good phone screen. You may find that they're not a good fit during the phone call.

› Respect the time and talent of all your candidates. Thank them for interviewing and let them know when you've extended an offer to someone else. You never know when you'll cross paths again.

Next Steps

After you bring aboard new marketing and sales employees, make sure that they understand your positioning, brand strategy and messaging so they can deliver on them every day.

Customer Relationship Management

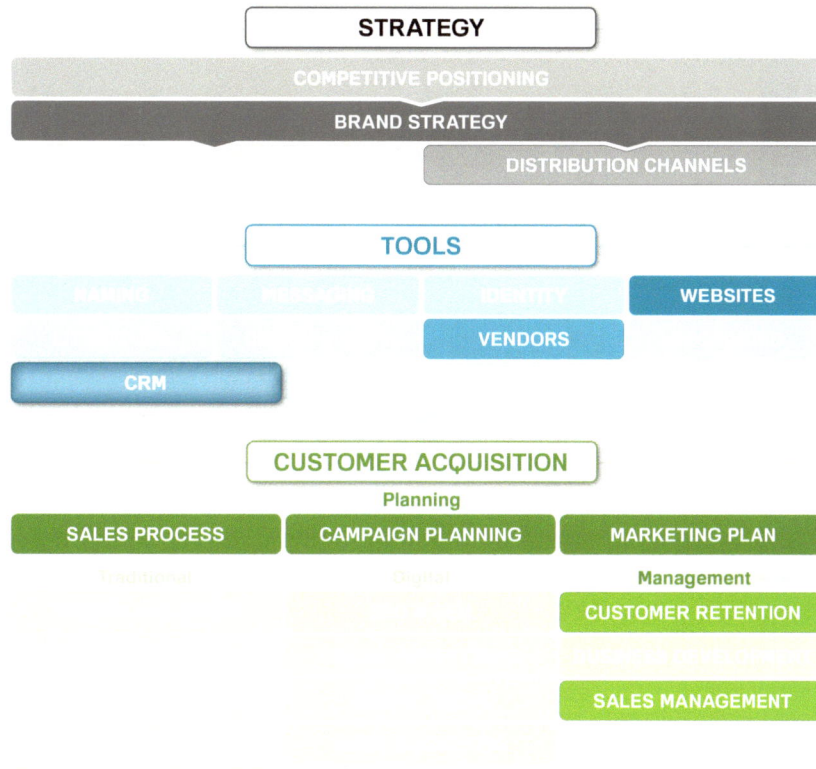

STRATEGY

COMPETITIVE POSITIONING
BRAND STRATEGY
DISTRIBUTION CHANNELS

TOOLS

BRANDING	MESSAGING	IDENTITY	WEBSITES
		VENDORS	
CRM			

CUSTOMER ACQUISITION

Planning

SALES PROCESS	CAMPAIGN PLANNING	MARKETING PLAN

Management

CUSTOMER RETENTION

SALES MANAGEMENT

Customer relationship management (CRM) is a term that refers to two things:

› A company's strategy for managing customer relationships and information
› Software that manages that data

In its simplest form, CRM is a database where sales, marketing and customer service teams store critical account data:

› Contact & account information (contact names, emails, phone numbers, SIC code, address, etc.)
› Lead information
› Sales rep name and activity history (calls, emails sent, inquiries, etc.)
› Purchase history
› Customer service tickets
› Sales pipeline information
› Marketing campaign data

CRM can also be an important reporting tool. For example, you can use it to:

› Generate revenue projections for a product, a sales rep, and your company as a whole
› Tie revenue to a marketing campaign
› Pull up lists of leads and activities by sales rep
› View the number of leads you have at each step in your sales process

> Track your progress against your goals
> Manage marketing campaigns
> Capture leads from your website
> Minimize the time your team spends creating manual sales & activity reports

Here are three examples of how different companies can use CRM:

Enterprise CRM	Mid-Market CRM	Small Company CRM
Company A is a national insurance company that sells direct to consumers and uses a single CRM system. Thousands of sales reps across the country log in, enter prospect data and use the system to manage their sales activities. At regional and corporate offices, many departments use the data to run-real time reports—revenue projections, sales metrics, customer growth, customer satisfaction, and ROI for marketing campaigns—to effectively manage the business.	Company B's 60 employees use CRM to manage 8,000 customer records and thousands of prospects. The system links to the "request information" form on the company's website. Leads are intelligently routed directly to the sales rep for that territory. The CRM links to the company's accounting software. When orders appear in the CRM system, they also appear in the appropriate financial reports. The operations team uses the system to fulfill orders and track shipping and service history.	Company C has four sales reps, two account managers and a marketing manager. They use a web-based system and pay per user per month. They started with a simple version and upgraded when they needed more functionality. Their system tracks leads by campaign, assigns leads to sales reps, tracks account activity, estimates revenue, launches and measures marketing campaigns, and stores templates for sales letters, emails and presentations.

Every company needs to store this information somewhere, and there are CRM products with very simple functionality, as well as complex multi-million dollar versions to handle almost any need. When you use the right CRM system, you gain knowledge and power to keep your team on track and measure progress against goals.

Best Case	Neutral Case	Worst Case
Your CRM matches your marketing, sales, customer service and retention strategies. It's easy to use and provides reports that eliminate the need to generate tedious manual reports. It integrates with other software like accounting and inventory, enabling your entire team to view important data and reports in real time.	Your CRM meets your basic needs. Your team uses it fairly regularly, but you have to keep on them to update data. It doesn't have all of the reporting capabilities that you'd like, and revenue reporting tends to be manual, so there's some lost sales productivity. It's fine, but it probably isn't the best solution.	You don't have a solid system for managing customer information—it's kept in various files or databases that aren't linked. It's difficult and time-consuming to create revenue projections, sales reports and marketing campaign reports. The result is lost revenue, productivity and opportunity.

How CRM Aligns with Strategy

When you define your positioning and brand strategies, part of your strategy might be to provide excellent customer service and build customer relationships. This would require a powerful CRM system.

SHARE
this ebook:

Key Concepts & Steps

Analyze your needs

If you're new to CRM or have a system that could be improved, define what you need.

› Decide what information your team should be able to access and how they'll use it.

› Identify who needs to use the system and where they're located (i.e. in different offices).

› Determine what reports you'll want to generate, particularly your revenue and pipeline reports.

› Identify the marketing programs that you'd like to be able to run and how that information can help you better manage your accounts.

If you've outgrown your current system, you may be able to purchase add-ins to give your existing system more power. You may also decide to evaluate new systems to gain the true functionality you need.

Evaluate and compare CRM software

Once you've defined your requirements, look for a CRM package that satisfies them. Remember that many systems come in several versions. You can start with a basic version and upgrade as you grow, but make sure the upgrade process is seamless.

Implement and monitor your system

When you're nearing the end of your selection process, prepare for implementation.

› Create an implementation team.

› Develop a schedule for key tasks: configuring fields, migrating data, creating reports, training users.

› Create a solid training plan.

› Launch the software.

› Perform follow-up training to ensure that your team uses the software as planned. Most implementations fail because employees don't use the software properly.

› Gather feedback and modify the software configuration as needed—make it as intuitive and powerful as possible.

Next Steps

Many CRM systems have evolved to include marketing modules that you can use in your marketing campaign execution. CRM software can dramatically improve your sales process and sales management, so make sure that your entire team understands how to effectively use the software.

Customer Lifetime Value

STRATEGY
COMPETITIVE POSITIONING
BRAND STRATEGY

TOOLS
NAMING	MESSAGING	IDENTITY	WEBSITES

CLV

CUSTOMER ACQUISITION
Planning

	CAMPAIGN PLANNING	MARKETING PLAN

Do you know what an average customer is truly worth to your company? By calculating your Customer Lifetime Value (CLV), you'll be able to answer that question.

CLV is the amount of profit that a customer delivers to your company for as long as the customer is buying from you. It's typically calculated as the net present value (the value in today's dollars) of the profit that you'll earn from all of a customer's purchases over time. When you know your CLV, you have an extremely powerful tool that helps with:

› **Acquisition:** You'll have a better understanding of what you can spend to acquire customers.

› **Targeting:** You'll know which customer segment delivers the most profit to your company and you can focus marketing efforts on that segment.

› **Return on investment:** By using CLV in your ROI calculations for marketing campaigns, you'll have a much more accurate measure of campaign performance.

› **Customer retention:** You can determine how much you can spend to profitably retain customers.

› **Single-customer profitability:** You can calculate the profitability of an individual customer.

CLV becomes more important as your marketing budget rises and your customer base grows. Yet even an early-stage company can benefit by using simple CLV estimates.

Best Case	Neutral Case	Worst Case
You know how much an average customer in each of your segments is worth to you. You focus your acquisition efforts on your most valuable segments, and you know how much you can spend to profitably retain your customers.	You have an idea of who your most valuable customers are, but you're not really sure how much you should spend to acquire or retain them. Your ROI measurements for your marketing campaigns are probably very general, though still helpful.	You don't know how much a customer is worth or how much you should spend on acquisition or retention. You're not sure what your marketing budget should be, and you're not confident in the quality of the investments you're making.

How CLV Aligns with Strategy

Knowing your customer lifetime value is helpful when evaluating your market segments to determine which are the most profitable. This information can be used when evaluating your positioning strategy to determine if you should strengthen your position within a particular segment or market, or target entirely new segments.

Key Concepts & Steps

Confirm your formulas

There are several figures you'll need for your CLV calculations:

› **Cost of goods sold (COGS):** the cost to physically produce a product or service
› **Gross profit:** the difference between the price of your product and the COGS

Companies calculate these figures differently, so your first step is to confirm the formulas your company uses.

Determine your customer segments

The CLV calculation is most valuable when you measure it by customer segment—similar groups of customers who use your products/services in a similar way.

For each segment, determine how long an average customer stays with you—their "lifetime"

Review your customers' buying patterns and calculate the total number of purchases they make and the time between those purchases.

Calculate your CLV for each segment

Once you know the average lifetime, you'll calculate:

› The total profit you earn on all of their purchases.
› The probability that they'll make successive purchases.
› The value of future revenue if you had the cash today.

DOWNLOAD hundreds of plans for these marketing activities at www.MarketingMO.com.

marketing MO

SHARE this ebook:

43

Use CLV to improve your acquisition and retention marketing

Once you have a CLV for each customer segment, you can:

› Set a maximum budget to acquire a particular type of customer.

› Calculate whether a particular deal will be profitable.

› Look at current customers who haven't purchased according to the pattern you estimated in the calculation. They're more likely to defect, so launch a retention campaign to those customers.

› Plug it into your ROI projections. It's more accurate to calculate your return on a campaign when you use the total profit the customer represents over time, not just the profit you earn on the first sale.

Next Steps

CLV is a powerful tool to use during the campaign planning process. Use it when projecting ROI before running a campaign, and after the campaign to see how well you performed.

It's also a valuable tool to use with customer retention, to determine how much to spend on your segments and customers, and when to let individual customers go.

Return on Investment

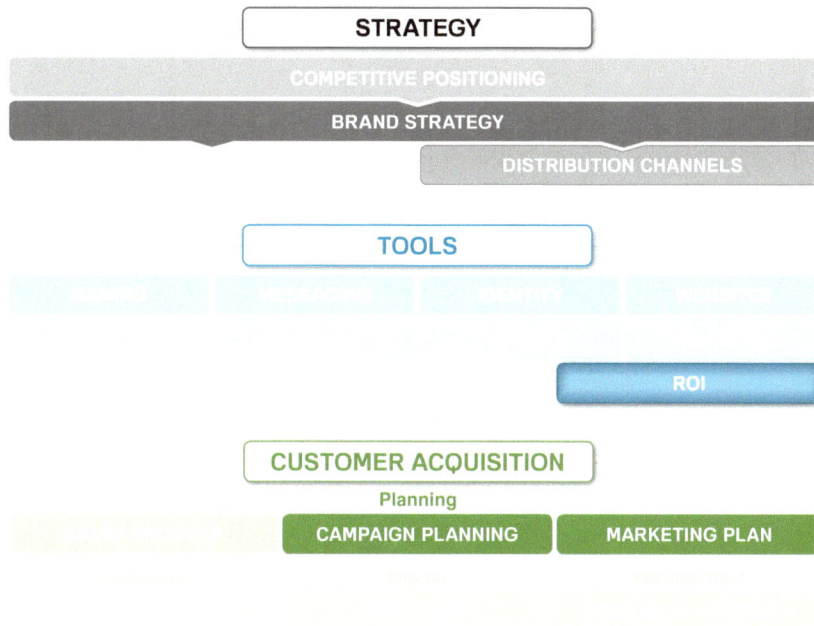

STRATEGY		
COMPETITIVE POSITIONING		
BRAND STRATEGY		
		DISTRIBUTION CHANNELS

TOOLS

ROI

CUSTOMER ACQUISITION

Planning

CAMPAIGN PLANNING	MARKETING PLAN

Marketing campaigns and initiatives are best treated as investments, not expenses. You're investing in enhancing your brand, building awareness, generating leads and driving sales. And like any smart investment, they should be measured, monitored and evaluated against other marketing investments to ensure that you're spending your money wisely.

Return on investment (ROI) is a measure of the profit earned from each investment. Like the "return" you earn on your portfolio or bank account, it's calculated as a percentage. In the simplest terms, the calculation is:

$$\frac{(Return - Investment)}{Investment}$$

To express it as a percentage, multiply your result by 100.

ROI calculations for marketing campaigns and initiatives can be complex. With many variables on both the return side and the investment (cost) side, understanding your ROI formula is essential in order to produce the best possible results.

For example, marketers may consider varied definitions of return, including:

> Total revenue (or gross receipts or turnover, depending on your organization type and location) defined as the top line sales generated from the campaign.

> Gross profit (or a gross profit estimate) defined as revenue minus the cost of goods to produce/deliver a product or service. Many marketers simply use the company's COG percentage (say 20%) and deduct it from the total revenue.

> Net profit, which is gross profit minus expenses.

On the investment side, it's easy for marketers to input the media costs as the investment. But what other costs should you include? When executing your campaign, you might include:

> Creative costs

> Printing costs

> Technical costs (such as email platforms and website coding)

> Management time

> Cost of sales

Basic Marketing ROI Formulas

One basic formula uses the gross margin for units sold in the campaign and the marketing investment for the campaign:

$$\frac{\text{Gross Profit} - \text{Marketing Investment}}{\text{Marketing Investment}}$$

You can also use the Customer Lifetime Value (CLV) instead of gross profit. CLV is a measure of the profit generated by a single customer or set of customers over their lifetime with your company.

$$\frac{\text{Customer Lifetime Value} - \text{Marketing Investment}}{\text{Marketing Investment}}$$

However, some companies deduct other expenses:

$$\frac{\text{Gross Profit (or CLV)} - \text{Marketing Investment} - *\text{Overhead Allocation} - *\text{Incremental Expenses}}{\text{Marketing Investment}}$$

These expenses are typically tracked in "Sales and General Expenses" in overhead, but some companies deduct them in ROI calculations to provide a closer estimate of the true profit that their marketing campaigns are generating for the company.

The components for calculating marketing ROI can be different for each organization, but with solid ROI calculations, you can focus on campaigns that deliver the greatest return. For example, if one campaign generates a 15% ROI and the other 50%, where will you invest your marketing budget next time? If your entire marketing budget only returns 6% and the stock market returns 12%, your company can earn more profit by investing in the stock market.

Understanding ROI helps you improve your ongoing campaigns. When you tweak your offer or launch a campaign using a different list, you can compare ROI and focus on the version with the best performance.

Finally, ROI helps you justify marketing investments. In tough times, companies often slash their marketing budgets—a dangerous move since marketing is an investment that produces revenue. By focusing on ROI, you can help your company move away from the idea that marketing is a fluffy expense that can be cut when times get tough.

Best Case	Neutral Case	Worst Case
You measure and track the ROI of all of your marketing investments. Your campaigns deliver the highest possible return and you're able to improve them over time. Your organization understands and agrees with the choices you make because there is solid data to support your investments.	You calculate ROI on some investments, but because it can get complex, you don't attempt to measure it at all times. You have a general idea of how your investments perform relative to each other, but you can't pinpoint the exact return you're generating. And in tough times, your budget is cut.	You don't measure the performance of any of your investments. In fact, marketing is viewed as a cost, rather than an investment. Your company isn't sure what works and what doesn't work, and it's a struggle to meet goals.

How ROI Aligns with Strategy

Return on investment calculations are powerful tools to use in campaign planning and execution. Use them to determine whether you can execute short-term marketing strategies profitably. ROI can be heavily influenced by the strength of your brand and your pricing. Strong brands can typically acquire customers at a lower cost than weak brands, increasing marketing ROI.

Key Concepts & Steps

Confirm your formulas

There are several figures you'll need for your ROI calculations:

> **Cost of goods sold (COGS):** The cost to physically produce a product or service.

> **Marketing investment:** Typically you'd include just the cost of the media, not production costs or time invested by certain employees. In certain cases, it may be better to include all of those figures.

> **Revenue:** It can be tricky to tie revenue to a particular campaign, especially when you run a variety of campaigns and have a long sales process. Your finance team may have some suggestions for estimating this figure.

Companies calculate these figures differently, so confirm the formulas your company uses—your finance team or accountant can guide you.

Establish an ROI threshold

Set an ROI goal for your entire budget and individual campaigns. Set a floor as well. By doing so, you gain more power over your budget. If you project that a campaign won't hit the threshold, don't run it. If you can't get an ongoing campaign over the threshold, cut it and put your money elsewhere.

Set your marketing budget

When you have an ROI goal and annual revenue/profit goals, you can calculate the amount of money you should spend on marketing—just solve the ROI formula for the "investment" figure. You'll be more confident that you're spending the right amount of money to meet your goals.

Calculate ROI on campaigns; track and improve your results

Tracking ROI can be tricky with complex marketing campaigns. With a commitment and a good reporting process, you can build solid measurements, even if you have to estimate during the process.

It's not feasible to track ROI on every marketing investment, though, as some, such as branding and PR are not worth the effort tracking. Many marketers simply separate their budget into two buckets—strategic spend, and campaign spending based on ROI projections.

Next Steps

By having a strong understanding of marketing ROI, you're able to better understand where to allocate your marketing budget—on the tools and campaigns that will produce a positive return.

Use your ROI calculations to continually improve your campaigns; test new ways to increase your ROI and spend your money on the campaigns that produce the greatest return for your company.

Sales Process

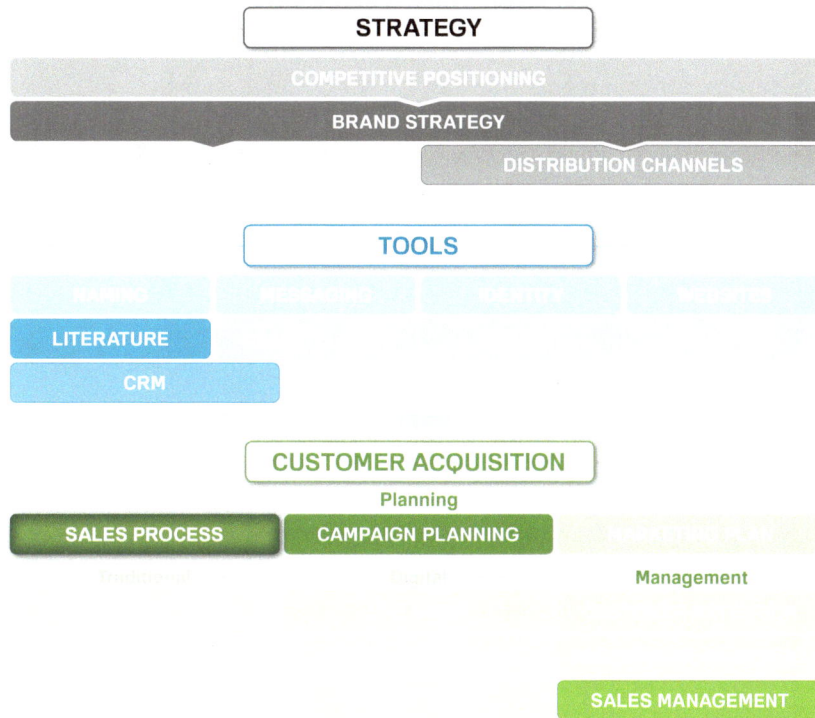

How do prospects decide to purchase your product or service? Does a single decision maker find your product or service and buy on the spot, or does s/he go through many steps and approvals first? Perhaps there are multiple people or departments involved in the decision, each with their own needs?

A sales process is a defined series of steps you follow as you guide prospects from initial contact to purchase. They're far more common in B2B than in B2C, but many high-ticket B2C items (such as real estate or autos) to have a distinct sales process.

Your sales process begins when you first identify a new prospect or the prospect engages with you. Here's an example:

Step 1	Step 2	Step 3	Step 4	Step 5
A prospect responds to a campaign and requests information.	A sales rep calls the prospect to explain your product.	An in-person meeting and product demo takes place.	Your team submits a proposal to the prospect.	The prospect signs an agreement and makes first payment.

A documented sales process is a flowchart that explains:

> Each distinct step a prospect takes

> Knowledge the prospect needs to move to the next step

> Literature and tools you provide to help the prospect move forward faster

> The length of time a prospect needs at each step

> Conversion rates: the percentage of prospects who move from one step to the next

With a documented sales process, you have a powerful tool that enables you to:

> Sell more efficiently

> Generate more accurate sales and revenue reports

> Estimate the revenue and return on investment (ROI) of your marketing campaigns

> See which stages take the most time and find new ways to move prospects forward

> Create better sales tools and literature

> Minimize the amount of time your reps spend on estimates and forecasts

Do you see your company in one of these scenarios?

Best Case	Neutral Case	Worst Case
You have a well-designed sales process that measures the number of prospects you have at each stage, how long they stay in each stage, and the revenue that your entire pipeline represents. You deliver the right amount of information that prospects need at each step, which helps them make decisions quickly and move to the next stage. You use your sales process to create more successful marketing campaigns because you can predict how many leads will become customers and what those leads will be worth to your company.	You may or may not have a defined sales process. You generally follow the same steps to create a customer, but there's a big variance in the amount of time it takes to close each one. In fact, even your strongest reps have trouble closing certain types of prospects. Your forecasts are probably all manual and generally accurate, but you wish that you had a reliable snapshot to show exactly how many accounts are at a certain stage and what you need to do to close.	You don't have a process or you use one that doesn't match how prospects want to buy. You deliver all of the information about your offering but then seem to lose control of the prospect. Some prospects end up buying, but you don't know why the others don't. It's a constant battle to figure out how many real prospects you have and what they're worth. Your sales team often spends valuable time creating manual reports instead of selling, which further hurts your marketing and sales performance.

How Sales Process Aligns with Strategy

If you have multiple distribution channels, you might find that you have a different sales process for each. And, you could have a different sales process for each offering you provide within an existing channel, so it's valuable to document the buying steps that your market prefers to take for each offering within each channel combination.

Your sales processes are also influenced by your positioning, brand strategy and pricing. Your brand personality should be evident at each step in the process. For example, if you're delivering a luxury experience, don't use pushy and aggressive sales tactics, and don't use price discounts to convert prospects to customers.

Key Concepts & Steps

Determine how your prospects buy

List the steps that you think prospects logically take from the time they recognize a problem to the time that they purchase a solution. Talk with customers or ask your sales reps for more insight. Figure out what steps they take, what they need to know at each step, and how you can deliver that information most effectively.

Create your process

For each step your prospects need to take, list:

› What the prospect needs to learn

› Sales tools and literature that you can provide to help the prospect move forward

› The length of time that a prospect needs at that step

› The percentage of prospects who move from each step to the next (your "conversion rate")

Integrate your process into your CRM

It's helpful to add each sales process to your customer relationship management (CRM) software so that each account is assigned to a stage at all times. That allows you to run reports to measure your progress and improve your sales management.

Project campaign results and revenue

When you have a sales process with conversion rates, you can quickly generate solid pipeline and revenue reports. For example, if you have 50 prospects at the presentation stage, your conversion metrics may show that 20% will become customers. That means those 50 prospects should deliver 10 new customers. Your conversion metrics will also tell you when that should happen and how much revenue those prospect represent.

You can use a similar calculation to project results from new marketing campaigns. For example, if a campaign should produce 100 qualified leads, you can estimate the number of meetings, presentations, and new customers that the campaign will generate.

Improve your process to maximize revenue

When you have a defined process, it's easier to test ideas for improving results. For example, you can:

› Identify spots where prospects get "stuck" in the process and try new materials or messages to help them move forward

› Measure how well different reps convert at each step and help those that aren't doing as well

› See how leads from different marketing campaigns convert, and use that information to improve your campaigns

› Create campaigns to "recycle" leads that fall out of the process at various spots

Next Steps

After you've documented your sales process, decide which sales tools and literature should be delivered at each step.

You'll also use your sales process in your sales management to measure the success of your marketing campaigns: for each campaign, you will be able to see how many leads entered the process and made it through each step.

Campaign Planning

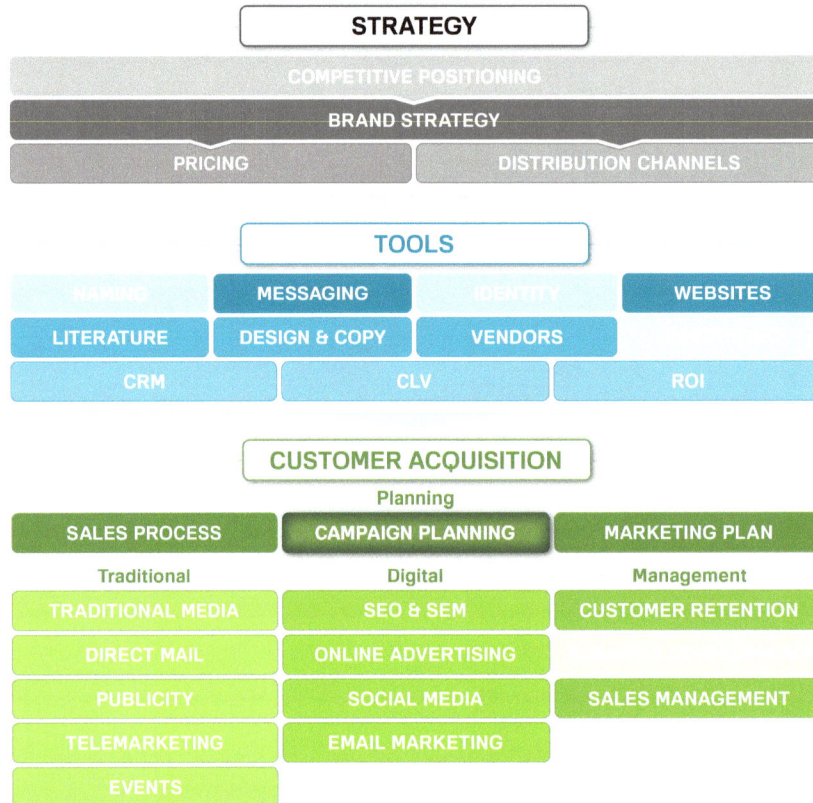

STRATEGY

COMPETITIVE POSITIONING	
BRAND STRATEGY	
PRICING	DISTRIBUTION CHANNELS

TOOLS

NAMING	MESSAGING	IDENTITY	WEBSITES
LITERATURE	DESIGN & COPY	VENDORS	
CRM	CLV		ROI

CUSTOMER ACQUISITION

Planning

SALES PROCESS	CAMPAIGN PLANNING	MARKETING PLAN
Traditional	Digital	Management
TRADITIONAL MEDIA	SEO & SEM	CUSTOMER RETENTION
DIRECT MAIL	ONLINE ADVERTISING	
PUBLICITY	SOCIAL MEDIA	SALES MANAGEMENT
TELEMARKETING	EMAIL MARKETING	
EVENTS		

For many companies, marketing campaigns are the main method for both communicating with their market to reinforce their positioning and for customer acquisition.

Good campaigns follow a theme and include a series of touches with the market. It's noisy in the marketplace, and a message delivered once through a single medium rarely makes a difference. While there's no magic number regarding the best frequency for a message to make an impact, opinions range from three to twenty times, with seven being an old marketing adage.

Many marketing campaigns contain an overarching theme, which can be leveraged over extended periods of time with multiple variations, or different elements, to tell an entire story.

An example would be The Duck campaign launched by the American Family Life Assurance Company in 2000. While the company had been in business since 1955, it had only a 12% brand recognition rate before the campaign launched. The company used the Kaplan Thaler Group to improve its name recognition. Kaplan created a new character, the Aflac Duck, who appeared in ads featuring customers who had trouble remembering the insurance company's name. In the ads, the duck appeared in the background and quacked the name "Aflac" (while usually ending up in a funny predicament).

You've seen them, right? As a result of the long-running campaign, Aflac's brand recognition jumped from 12% to 90%, and increased sales catapulted Aflac into a leadership position in the supplemental insurance market.

SHARE
this ebook:

Large consumer marketers typically use ad agencies (both traditional media and digital media agencies) to design their campaign creative, handle the media buys, and track results. These are often multi-million dollar endeavors, and have brought us such memorable advertising campaigns as:

› "Just Do It" – Nike

› "The Most Interesting Man in the World" – Dos Equis

› "Where's the Beef?" – Wendy's

› "We Try Harder" – Avis

› "Absolutely, Positively Overnight" – FedEx

While most small- to mid-market companies can't afford the multi-million dollar ad budgets from the Madison Avenue agencies, they can create effective and memorable campaigns leveraging different media such as:

› Online media, including interactive ads and banners on website

› Print media

› Social media

› Publicity

› Direct mail

› Email

› Radio

› Television

› Telemarketing

› Events and trade shows

› Search engines

› Outdoor media

True marketing campaigns are more than just advertisements. Complex campaigns leverage multiple mediums, use a sequence of messages over an extended timeframe, support positioning, define a brand experience, and handle the campaign fulfillment and selling.

Campaigns can also be simple—using a single medium, with a single message and call-to-action. Here are three examples of very simple campaigns:

Generate New Leads	Drive Existing Prospects to Your Trade Show Booth & VIP Reception	Promote an Offer for a Special Occasion
1. Use a paid search ad promotion with a special theme or call-to-action to generate traffic to your website. 2. Receive information requests from prospects via a landing page form. 3. Email the requested information. 4. Call the prospect; qualify the prospect further and determine next steps.	1. Mail a postcard to attendees 3 weeks before the show; invite them to your booth with an intriguing incentive. 2. Mail a special invite to key prospects and customers for a VIP reception. Ask them to RSVP by phone, email or URL. 3. Call key prospects and customers as a second effort. 4. Send an email to all confirmed attendees 3 days before the event. 5. Email the non-respondents one last time.	1. Run banner ads on industry websites and targeted email newsletters, driving traffic to a special landing page to take advantage of a special offer such as a sale, or free promotion. 2. Send out a special email to your house list to promote the offer. 3. Create an intriguing story and tie it to your offer. Write a search-optimized press release and post it on your site; distribute the release and pitch the story to a key industry reporter. 4. Run paid search ads driving traffic to the landing page.

It's good practice to start with your company's annual goals and work backwards to develop campaigns to meet those numbers. For example, when you know how many new customers you need, you can calculate how many leads you'll need, and then design campaigns to generate that number of leads over the course of the year.

With solid planning, a jolt of creativity, and a focus on measurement, you'll be in a strong position for success.

Best Case	Neutral Case	Worst Case
You plan and execute your campaigns to hit specific goals. You don't always hit them, but you test and improve different elements; the ROI on your overall budget is above your goal. You focus on an offer and call-to-action, and you touch your prospects several times and follow up when appropriate. You recognize the challenges in measuring results, but you do what you can; it helps you improve the next time around.	Your campaigns aren't the most creative or the splashiest, but you've hit many of your marketing goals. You don't test, but your response rate is fine. You don't know your ROI, but you know generally which campaigns work best. When you're faced with ambitious annual goals, you have problems gaining budget approval. Since you stick with the same campaigns, year in and year out, it's also difficult to figure out how to generate additional leads.	Your marketing programs tend to be reactive—suddenly you're low on leads or falling short of your goals and you launch a campaign to fix the problem. Since your programs don't seem to work, it's difficult to gain budget approval for future campaigns that could be better-planned and executed. It's a vicious cycle and you don't know how to get out of it.

How Campaign Planning Aligns with Strategy

Your marketing campaigns are the vehicles for connecting with your marketplace, to generate leads and sales, and to position you as that certain "something."

Campaign copy and creative should always support your brand strategy and messages, even if you're running a tactical lead generation campaign. They're one of the most effective customer acquisition tactics in your marketing arsenal.

Key Concepts & Steps

Quantify your goals

› Plan your campaigns to meet your annual revenue and volume goals. For example, if you're trying to generate 100 new customers, use your sales process conversion rates to figure out how many leads you'll need and when you'll need them.

› Think about how you'll use different media. For example, if you're B2B, your sales team may be able to generate 30% of your leads through prospecting; the rest may come from telemarketing, email, social media, direct mail, search marketing, webinars, trade shows, etc.

Generate campaign ideas and strategies

› Identify all of the business goals that will need marketing support. You may need campaigns to generate and nurture prospects, to sell direct or through a channel, or to market to existing customers.

› Evaluate ideas and options (traditional sales activities, Internet marketing, social media, telemarketing, direct mail, email and publicity) to determine which ones are most effective for meeting a particular goal.

Target your audience

› With more specific targeting, you can speak more directly to the prospect and raise your response rates in the process.

Deliver one or two key messages and your call-to-action

› If you include every detail about your offering, it's easy for prospects to become overwhelmed. Move a prospect just one step at a time.

› Be creative—your market is bombarded with messages daily, so grab their attention and engage them.

Create your budget and estimate your return on investment

Projecting campaign ROI is a powerful exercise that forces you to think through and estimate results for the important metrics of your campaign:

› Impressions, or exposure to your campaign creative

› Conversions, or those who take action from the impression

› The steps required to move from a conversion to a customer

› The number of units sold, and the profit from each

› The items of your campaign budget

› The estimated ROI of your campaign

Plan your fulfillment

› Your fulfillment processes can help or hurt your close rate, so be sure you outline your requirements. For example, if you're running a campaign where prospects request a software demo, and it doesn't arrive for a week, your prospects may lose interest.

Plan to measure

When you measure your campaigns, it's easier to gain budget approval the next time around. You'll also know exactly which programs produce the highest return.

› Establish how you'll measure the success of each campaign. If there are variables you can't measure, decide how you will account for those results.

› Identify how you'll capture the data you need to track responses to your campaign—unique phone numbers, unique URLs, etc.

Continually test and improve

› Even on a small campaign, you can evaluate your ad, your copy, your list or other factors before you spend your entire budget.

› Choose a subset of your list or two versions of an ad; test them in small quantities and choose the best one for rollout. Then you can test a second variable against the winner of the first test.

› Keep the testing cycle going and track your results over time. You'll improve your response rates and your return on investment.

Next Steps

After you plan your campaign, it's time to focus on tactical execution. That means having a deep understanding of the media you're using, carefully planning your media buys, tracking your results, and following the best practices and steps for each media you use.

Marketing Plan & Budget

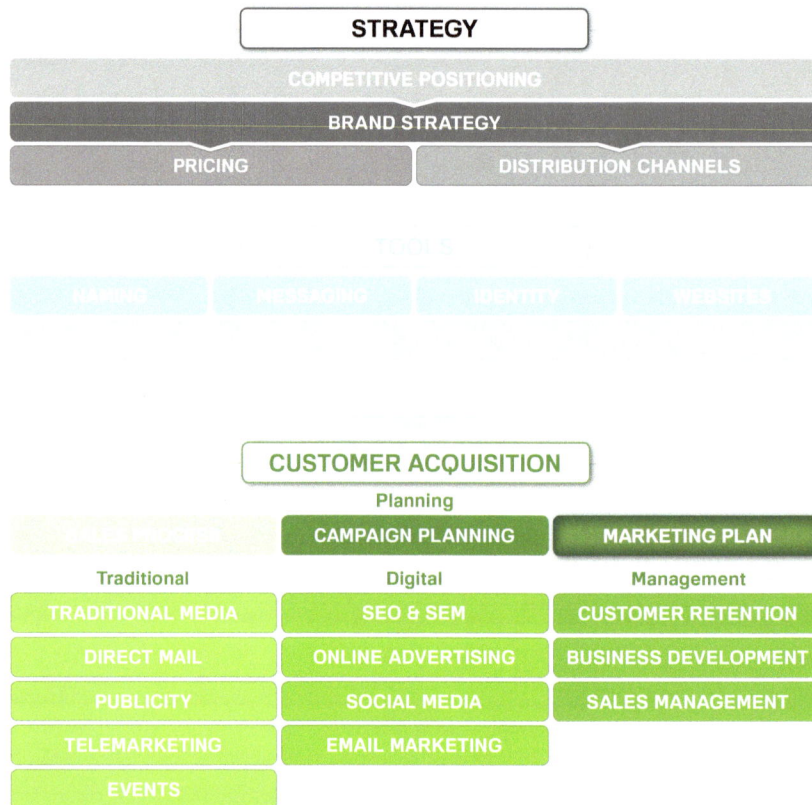

STRATEGY		
COMPETITIVE POSITIONING		
BRAND STRATEGY		
PRICING	DISTRIBUTION CHANNELS	

TOOLS

NAMING	MESSAGING	IDENTITY	WEBSITES

CUSTOMER ACQUISITION

Planning

CAMPAIGN PLANNING	MARKETING PLAN

Traditional	Digital	Management
TRADITIONAL MEDIA	SEO & SEM	CUSTOMER RETENTION
DIRECT MAIL	ONLINE ADVERTISING	BUSINESS DEVELOPMENT
PUBLICITY	SOCIAL MEDIA	SALES MANAGEMENT
TELEMARKETING	EMAIL MARKETING	
EVENTS		

A marketing plan is a detailed roadmap that outlines all of your marketing strategies, tactics, costs and projected results over a period of time. The plan keeps your entire team focused on specific goals—it's a critical resource for your entire company.

A good marketing plan typically includes:

- Positioning strategy
- Brand strategy
- Product/service overview
- Detailed goals by product, distribution channel and/or customer segment

- Sales plan
- Major marketing campaigns
- Detailed budget
- Dates to review progress

It takes time to develop a solid plan, but it's important because it ties all of your activities to tangible goals. It's also a great opportunity to focus on the future, generate new ideas, and inspire your team. Even a simple plan is better than none, but when you invest more effort upfront, you'll have a better roadmap toward your goals.

Best Case	Neutral Case	Worst Case
Your marketing plan is a detailed roadmap to meet your goals. You recognize that the time you invest to create a solid plan is perhaps the best time you'll invest all year—it helps you work through new strategies, issues, ideas and numbers. When it's done, your team focuses on executing the plan and measuring your progress all year long. As a result, you've been able to hit your goals, grow your business, and enjoy the journey.	You're incredibly busy, so it's difficult to invest the time in a detailed marketing plan. Instead, you develop a basic plan that's based on last year's version. You include general revenue goals, general sales strategies, and basic campaigns; you stick with proven techniques. Budgets are based on last year's numbers. You could be more ambitious with your revenue goals if your company was willing to try new things, but each year you stick with the tried-and-true.	You don't typically create a marketing plan. You have a budget, but the numbers are haphazard. Things change so quickly—why spend the time? You take a similar approach with the strategies that should drive a marketing plan. You probably don't have a positioning or brand strategy; you're missing out on distribution channels or partnerships; your campaigns are ineffective and you may not invest in customer retention. A plan is a compass. Without one, you may be traveling in the right direction, but it's incredibly difficult to stay on course—and that can drastically limit your success.

How Your Marketing Plan and Budget Align with Strategy

Some statistics have shown that up to 85% of small- to mid-size companies create an annual marketing budget, but without a concrete plan to accompany it. This explains why so many marketers are tactically focused—they're figuring out how to spend a defined budget, instead of thinking about goals and strategies.

Creating an annual marketing plan, if done properly, forces you to think through your positioning and brand strategy, along with your pricing, distribution, sales and customer retention strategies.

After outlining your strategies and setting your goals, begin outlining campaign ideas to bring your strategies to life. Writing a comprehensive marketing plan can be a challenging exercise for many, but it's a powerful one that is worth investing in.

Key Concepts & Steps

Set your annual goals

Build your entire marketing plan to achieve the goals that you define:

› Quantitative (numeric) goals such as total revenue, profit, number of customers, units sold, and breakdowns by product or channel as needed.
› Strategic goals—for example, you may want to expand into a new market with a new distribution channel, or you may need to reposition your brand to reflect a change in your business.

Emphasize your positioning in the marketplace

› Your positioning strategy defines how you'll differentiate your offering from those of your competitors.
› Your brand strategy defines what you stand for and how you'll communicate with the market.

Outline any plans for product or service improvements

If you need to do anything to strengthen your product line and better deliver on your positioning, address those issues in your plan.

Develop your tactical sales plan

› The number of sales reps you'll need and the markets they'll target

› Whether you'll need to develop new compensation plans, or hire and train new personnel

› Top priority markets, industries or customer segments; if you have a list of key prospects, include them

› Your plan for managing current customers

› Plans for launching any new distribution channels and driving revenue through existing channels

Outline your major marketing campaigns

You don't need to list every campaign—just outline your major promotional plans for the year. You'll need to set your budget too, so the more planning you do now, the better. Your plans should include:

› The top three campaigns you'll run to generate leads, nurture customers, close, and/or market to existing customers

› The media you'll use (for example, email, social, online, print, telemarketing, trade shows, publicity, etc.)

› Tools, technologies or resources you'll need—for example, a new website, an email service provider, or a new piece of software

› Your estimated ROI and other financial goals

Develop a budget

› Budgeting can be a difficult process. Many companies just estimate or base it on their previous year's spend. An estimate is better than nothing, but if you've defined your major campaigns and needs, you can develop better numbers.

› You can use ROI to determine the appropriate total budget for your marketing efforts.

Revisit your plan regularly

› The planning process itself is immensely valuable, but if you don't review the plan regularly, it's easy to lose focus. Periodically revisit the plan, and measure your progress.

Next Steps

When you've finished your plan, it's time to execute. You may need to create new messages, literature, websites or other tools and processes for your campaigns, but after that, focus on customer acquisition.

Traditional Media

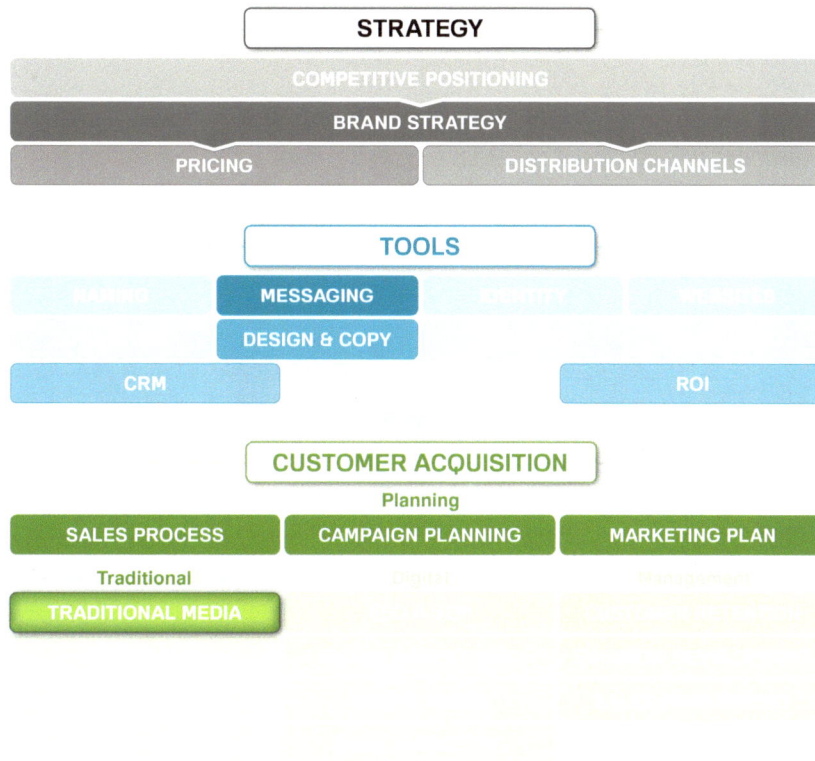

STRATEGY		
COMPETITIVE POSITIONING		
BRAND STRATEGY		
PRICING		DISTRIBUTION CHANNELS

TOOLS		
	MESSAGING	
	DESIGN & COPY	
CRM		ROI

CUSTOMER ACQUISITION

Planning

SALES PROCESS	CAMPAIGN PLANNING	MARKETING PLAN

Traditional

TRADITIONAL MEDIA

Marketers have used traditional media such as print, radio, TV, yellow pages and even outdoor ads to reach consumer markets for the last 50 to 100 years.

Traditional media can also play a role in the marketing mix for many B2B companies. These media often reach a broad audience and thus can be relatively expensive. Yet in your industry or region, they may be very effective in helping you reach your market. For example:

> In many industries, print ads in monthly trade journals are an important vehicle to reach decision makers.

> If your company sells to a certain geographic region, directory listings and ads may be crucial for reaching buyers when they're searching for solutions.

> You may need to reach a wide variety of prospects in different industries, so you may advertise in a regional or national business publication, newspaper or radio program.

You can use these media to generate leads, build visibility, share your message and/or drive specific promotions. They're especially helpful when you use them in conjunction with other media in a larger campaign.

DOWNLOAD hundreds of plans for these marketing activities at www.MarketingMO.com.

marketing MO

SHARE this ebook:

59

Here are two sample campaigns that incorporate traditional media:

Use Print & Online to Generate Leads	Use Radio to Generate Leads & Awareness
To generate leads, you run a print ad in an industry journal and a banner ad on the publication's website and in their monthly subscriber email. The prospect calls to take advantage of your offer, or visits a unique landing page on your website and fills out a form. A sales rep calls and sets up an in-person presentation.	You run a schedule of :30 ads on a talk radio show that reaches a broad base of businesspeople in your industry or region. As part of your package, you buy exclusive sponsorship of the show. You receive special mentions throughout the show, and you use the entire campaign to drive traffic to a specific landing page on your website. The page continues your message, captures the prospect's information or encourages a phone call. Your telemarketing team qualifies leads and transfers hot prospects to your sales team.

It's important to treat these programs as longer-term investments because responses tend to come in gradually—they aren't as immediate or measurable as internet marketing, telemarketing or direct mail. Targeting may be an issue and you may not be able to measure the branding impact of your campaign, but they're solid vehicles when they're in line with your goals or used in a larger campaign.

Best Case	Neutral Case	Worst Case
You understand the strengths and limitations of traditional media, and you use them effectively in campaigns to drive awareness and response. You test your campaigns to improve them over time and you measure the campaigns to the best of your ability. While you don't measure the value of your brand-building, you do adjust your ROI calculations to incorporate an allowance for that value.	You run a sprinkling of traditional media campaigns and generally track the number of responses that they generate. You know they work to some degree, but you can't quantify the results. The ads themselves are mediocre, but you rarely test them to improve. You know it's important to be in the vehicles you choose, and you stick with the same tactics because your competitors are doing the same thing.	You don't evaluate your media buys very carefully. You don't have specific goals and thus can't measure whether you're successful or not. You don't really test your ads either—they offer a lot of information and you can't really say whether they work either for branding or direct response. You're wasting your budget and time on programs that could be vastly improved.

How Traditional Media Aligns with Strategy

Campaigns using traditional media should support your positioning and brand strategy, contributing to the experience that you wish to deliver and the mindshare that you wish to own.

Additionally, make sure that your traditional media campaign is aligned to the goals that you've established in your campaign plan.

SHARE
this ebook:

Key Concepts & Steps

Develop a strong strategy

First, determine what you need to accomplish. For example, you may need to generate a specific number of leads, raise your visibility in a certain industry or geography, or communicate a key message across different media. Set tangible goals for your traditional media plan.

Each traditional media vehicle has benefits and drawbacks. When you've defined your goals, you can decide which vehicle will work best. Make sure you plan how to measure your campaign as well.

Decide whether to buy media in-house or through an agency

Media buying can be a tricky and time-consuming process. If you have a lot of media to buy, you may want to hire an agency. You'll pay for their services, but they may also have more buying power to negotiate better deals and find ways to reach your target market more cost-effectively.

Consider targeting when comparing costs

Media sales reps may quote you a flat rate for a particular ad or they may quote a cost per thousand (CPM) impressions. You may pay a higher CPM for a more targeted media than a general one, but if you calculate your cost per targeted impression instead, you can truly compare apples to apples.

Create a compelling ad and call-to-action

Your ad needs to grab the attention of your market—be creative, but keep your message simple and clear. Include a call-to-action—encourage prospects to call or visit a special landing page to learn more about a particular offer or program.

Continually test, refine and improve

It's wise to test any campaign before spending your entire budget. If you're considering multiple publications for print ads, run the same ad in two different ones to see which generates the best response. Or test different headlines and offers. Your goal is to find the ads and publications that generate the best response, and then run them for the remainder of your campaign.

Next Steps

As you design and manage campaigns using traditional media, evaluate the effectiveness of the tools used in the campaign, measure your results, and focus on continuous improvement.

Direct Mail

STRATEGY

COMPETITIVE POSITIONING

BRAND STRATEGY

PRICING | DISTRIBUTION CHANNELS

TOOLS

NAMING | MESSAGING | IDENTITY | WEBSITES

DESIGN & COPY

CRM | ROI

CUSTOMER ACQUISITION

Planning

SALES PROCESS | CAMPAIGN PLANNING | MARKETING PLAN

Traditional | Digital | Management

DIRECT MAIL

For many years, direct mail has been an important marketing vehicle. Even though many companies have turned to email and internet marketing, a targeted and well-produced mail campaign can still be highly effective.

Direct mail campaigns can generate leads, promote special offers, support other campaigns, communicate with customers and raise your visibility in your market. You can be very simple or wildly creative depending on your goals—for example, you can use a:

> Handwritten note

> Simple but effective sales letter

> Postcard with a four-color image on one side and a printed message on the back

> Digitally-printed brochure with the prospect's name printed in the headline and body copy

> Dimensional piece that you develop for a specific purpose

Direct mail can be an effective vehicle for a B2B company if you focus on strategic, targeted mailings instead of large bulk mail campaigns, which draw very low response rates at much higher costs than online marketing. Instead, consider using mail to:

> Invite current customers and top prospects to an event you're holding at a trade show

> Send product literature with the prospect's name and custom specifications printed into the brochure itself (via digital printing)

> Announce a compelling sale

Here are three sample mail campaigns:

Generate New Leads	Nurture Existing Leads	Cross-Sell Current Customers
Mail a personalized, hand-signed letter to targeted prospects. Quickly introduce your value proposition; invite prospects to call or visit your website to view a demo, download a special report, or request a quote. Follow up with a phone call a week later.	Mail a quarterly "industry update" or case study with graphs and reference info—more than you'd be able to provide in an email newsletter. Focus the piece on a typical objection prospects have before they buy.	Develop a piece that delivers a compelling case for your current customers to buy related products and services. Include a strong call-to-action; encourage customers to call or visit your website to learn more and buy.

If you're B2B, it's better to think about mail as an integral part of a larger campaign. Don't just mail and wait for the phone to ring. Instead, plan a campaign that starts with an introduction via mail, then perhaps a follow-up phone call from a sales rep and a demo delivered via email or via social media.

When you use the right strategy and execution, direct mail can be a strong addition to your marketing arsenal.

Best Case	Neutral Case	Worst Case
You're happy with the ROI on your mail campaigns. You design each piece to grab attention, convey a simple message and move the prospect toward action. You test your mailings and tweak the headlines, envelopes or offers to increase response, and you use targeted and current lists.	You've had some success with mail campaigns. Sometimes they're spur-of-the moment; you know that you could do a better job of planning ahead and focusing your message. You typically use mail in conjunction with a phone call. You don't really test your campaigns and try to improve results, but your response rates are acceptable.	You've used mail in the past but felt that it was a waste of money. The list was expensive and didn't necessarily have the right contact names. The mail piece and postage were expensive and contained a lot of information, yet it didn't generate the response you planned. You had counted on it generating a lot of leads that you ended up having to find elsewhere.

How Direct Mail Aligns with Strategy

Campaigns using direct mail should support your positioning and brand strategy, contributing to the experience that you wish to deliver and the mindshare that you wish to own.

Additionally, make sure that your direct mail campaign is tied to the goals you've established in your campaign plan.

Key Concepts & Steps

Define your goals

Tie your campaign to a specific objective—for example, the number of responses that you need or the number of customers you want to generate. Then design your campaign to meet your specific goal.

Target your audience

Narrow your audience as much as you can—you'll be able to speak more directly to your prospects with better results. You'll also save on postage and production.

Focus on the offer

Don't overwhelm your audience with every detail about your product and company. Focus on the offer itself—the purpose for the mailing, the call-to-action. For example, if you're promoting a software demo, explain what the demo will help them learn and why they should request it now. Touch on the key benefits, but don't muddy your message by including every detail about the software and the history of your company.

Develop your content, then your creative

First determine how much copy you'll need, what kind of graphics or photography you'll include, how to promote the offer, etc. Once you've defined the content you'll need to achieve your goals, start the design process. If you're working with a design and/or writing team, explain your requirements in a creative brief so you're all on the same page.

Tackle the campaign logistics

Make sure that you plan how your piece will be folded, stuffed, addressed, stamped, mailed, etc. If you're running large campaigns, you may want to hire a vendor to handle this step.

Test, measure and continually improve

Mail is a terrific media for testing—you can select a random set of records from your list, send your mailing, measure your response, then tweak the mailing and send it to another subset. You can improve the list targeting, your offer, the envelope design, the copy and the design itself. Commit to continuous improvement and use what you learn in all future campaigns.

Next Steps

As you design and manage campaigns using direct mail, evaluate the effectiveness of the tools used in the campaign, and focus on continually improving your tactical execution.

SHARE
this ebook:

Publicity

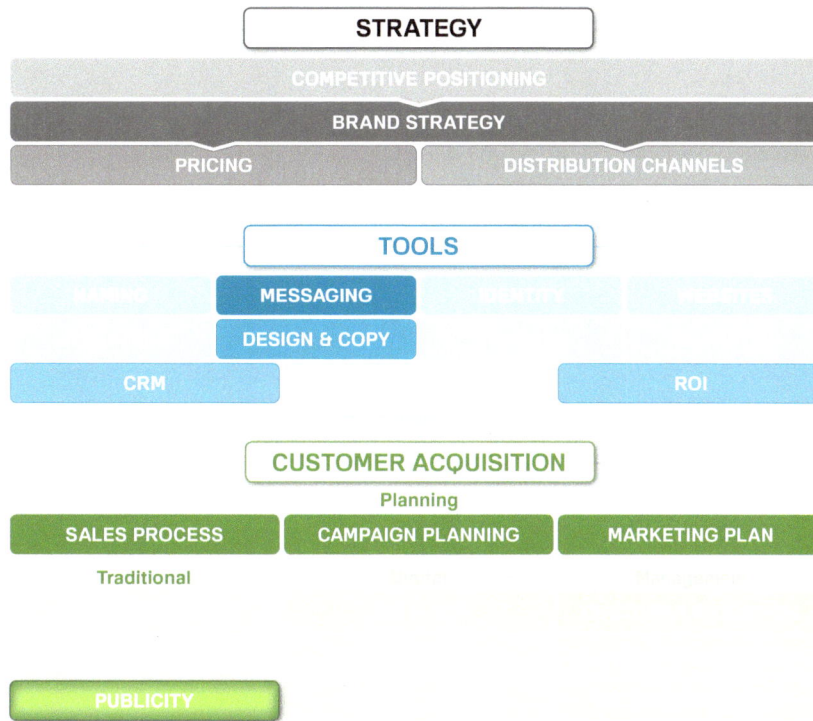

Have you ever read a story about a company and then contacted them to learn more about their product or service? Or listened to a CEO deliver a speech and found yourself researching the company later on?

Publicity in the media can be extremely valuable in building credibility and awareness for your company, product or service. For example, a legitimate news story acts as an endorsement that can reach a wide audience for very little cost beyond your own creativity and time. There are many forms of publicity including:

› News stories and interviews in trade journals, industry sites, newspapers, magazines, etc.
› "Expert" quotes in a story written by a journalist or blogger
› Self-authored stories published on websites or in industry publications
› Speaking engagements

Publicity is a cost-effective medium that can:

› Build awareness about your brand, products or services, expertise and people
› Drive prospects to your website
› Drive event attendance or participation in a promotion
› Educate the market about problems your company can solve
› Create an ongoing dialogue with the market

The key to success: create newsworthy stories. They should be interesting, relevant and timely. They should educate and inform, and provide your prospects with insight into how to solve a problem.

Even if you don't think you have newsworthy content to share with the world, you can benefit by implementing small newsworthy programs (such as charity work) that will raise your visibility. At the very least, you should include news releases on your website; they help improve search engine rankings and enable prospects to see what you've been doing.

Publicity isn't about luck—it's about investing in a good PR program, and it can really pay off over time.

Best Case	Neutral Case	Worst Case
Your company is very well known in your industry. When you launch a product or release a newsworthy story, important publications write about you, and you're often quoted in industry articles. You capitalize on the role the Internet plays in publicity—your press releases drive prospects and customers to your website. You also use blogs or other online publicity techniques to create a strong presence on the Internet.	You use PR sporadically with mixed results—an occasional blurb in an industry journal, a miscellaneous quote as an expert. You put press releases on your website and distribute them online, knowing that they make your site more interesting to prospects, but you're not sure whether you're gaining the full benefit from your efforts.	You don't use any form of public relations. You may be a startup or an established company, but you're not known by journalists in your industry. You see your competitors featured in industry publications even when your solution may be better; your company doesn't seem to have that level of credibility, and you're not sure how to get it.

How Publicity Aligns with Strategy

Campaigns using publicity should support your positioning and convey your brand's personality.

Additionally, make sure that your publicity campaign is tied to the goals that you've established in your campaign plan.

Key Concepts & Steps

Create a publicity strategy

Don't just "shotgun" press releases when you need to drum up some attention. Plan your publicity strategy as you would any marketing campaign:

› Develop a calendar that ties story ideas to key events and spreads your content out over the year.
› List events that may offer good speaking opportunities.
› Identify publications, reporters and bloggers who cover subjects that are relevant for your company.
› Create traditional and online press materials to give reporters supporting and background information for their stories.
› Know the audience for each story and carefully target your media.

Develop newsworthy story ideas

Every day, journalists are bombarded with press releases touting new product launches, business alliances, research discoveries, etc. But journalists don't just make announcements—they need to tell compelling stories that their readers will find interesting and useful. A trade journal may run a one-paragraph blurb about a new product, but to get headlines, photos, interviews and full-page coverage, you need to develop real stories.

Like movies, good news stories are often about conflict. An endless stream of positive information is boring. Instead, develop stories with substance: Good vs. Evil, Nature vs. Nurture, Race Against Time, Company A vs. Company B, Employee Against the World, Company vs. the System.

In addition, good stories can "go viral" when you distribute them on the web.

Market your stories and expertise

Journalists need stories. When you have a story, you have something to offer. With a quick, courteous phone call and a simple pitch, you may find a journalist who says, "Yes, I'm interested in that story, send me your material." That three-minute phone call could make a substantial difference in your campaign success.

Reach out when you identify a potential speaking engagement or find a journalist or blogger who may want to quote an expert from your company. Be sure to prepare a short pitch and support materials as well.

Use the Internet

Many PR experts say the traditional press release is dead. These days, a worthwhile PR strategy has to capitalize on the Internet.

› Write a second version of your normal releases with rich keywords and a format that helps search engines easily find the release.

› Post your search-friendly releases on your site—they should be represented as an actual page on the site, not a PDF.

› Send your release to Internet news distribution services.

› Consider adding an RSS feed to your site—it will send updated content to other publishers.

› Distribute your releases via Twitter, Facebook, Digg and other social media sites.

Next Steps

As you design and manage publicity campaigns, evaluate the effectiveness of the tools used in the campaign, and focus on continually improving your tactical execution.

It's difficult to measure the return on publicity, but if you're really focused on creating stories and reaching out, you have sound potential for success. One big story or important speaking engagement could generate fantastic results, so keep at it!

DOWNLOAD hundreds of plans for these marketing activities at www.MarketingMO.com.

marketing MO

SHARE this ebook:

67

Telemarketing

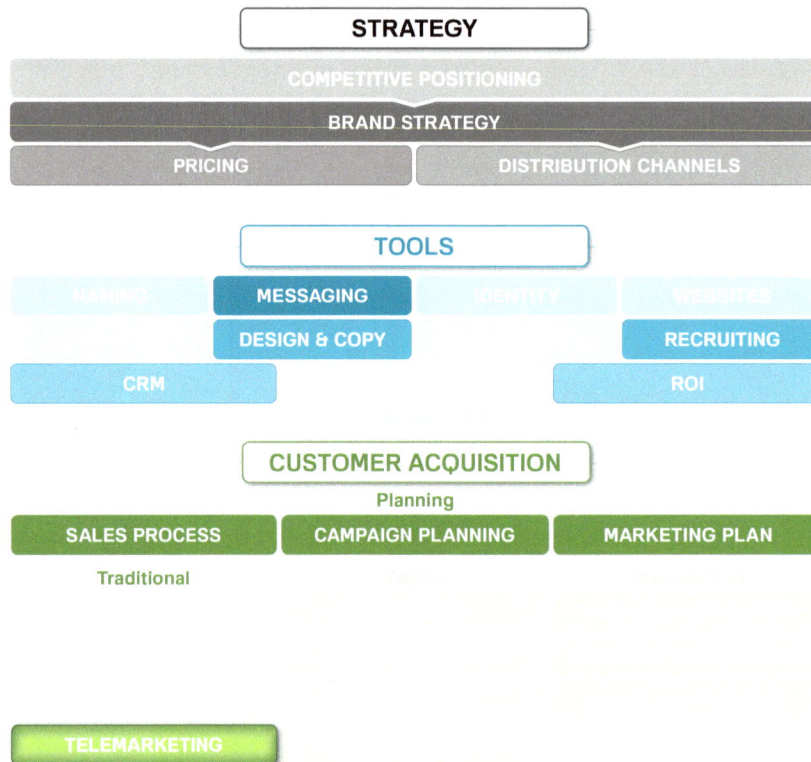

STRATEGY

COMPETITIVE POSITIONING

BRAND STRATEGY

PRICING | DISTRIBUTION CHANNELS

TOOLS

NAMING | MESSAGING | IDENTITY | WEBSITES

DESIGN & COPY | RECRUITING

CRM | ROI

CUSTOMER ACQUISITION

Planning

SALES PROCESS | CAMPAIGN PLANNING | MARKETING PLAN

Traditional

TELEMARKETING

The phrase "cold calling" sends chills down the spines of many businesspeople. It's often viewed as an intimidating, difficult, and boring process . . . and that means it doesn't get done as often as it should.

Telemarketing campaigns help companies reach a group of targeted prospects or customers to communicate a message, gather feedback, and determine a next step for the relationship. Telemarketing can be an important part of any marketing strategy—for example, you can use it to:

› Generate leads
› Qualify prospects who have downloaded information from your website or attended a webinar
› Follow up on a direct mail or email offer
› Take orders for special promotions
› Keep your marketing database current
› Conduct marketing research

In many companies, sales reps should make hundreds or thousands of cold calls every month to set appointments and/or generate leads. But busy reps usually prefer to work on closing their existing pipeline. Prospecting often slips on the priority list; as a result, the sales pipeline isn't always filled with new prospects.

If cold calling is an effective way to introduce your company to new prospects, don't ignore it. Instead of forcing a sales team to devote time to prospecting, many companies use an in-house or outsourced telemarketing group to make a high volume of calls, find decision makers and qualify leads for the field sales group.

When telemarketers handle prospecting, salespeople can spend 100% of their time selling and closing. Your company can produce more revenue in the same amount of time; your reps earn more commission, they're doing what they love, and they're more satisfied with their jobs.

You can use a telemarketing team in a variety of campaigns:

Outbound Lead Generation	Outbound Campaign Support	Inbound Sales Support
Company A's telemarketers call targeted lists. They identify the decision maker, ask qualifying questions, and gauge the prospect's needs and interest level. If a prospect meets certain criteria, the telemarketer sets a follow-up appointment for a sales rep.	Company B increases their response rates by including a phone call in campaigns. For example, when they hold an event at a trade show, they call prospects before mailing an invite to lift their response rate. They also follow up with those who don't respond.	Company C makes sure that prospects who visit their website can call and speak with someone immediately. They use an inbound sales support team to answer questions and probe callers. The reps send follow-up materials and a field sales rep follows up with the most qualified prospects.

With the right strategy and proper management, a good telemarketing operation can produce great value for your company.

Best Case	Neutral Case	Worst Case
You have a team or vendor to prequalify leads and handle inbound and outbound calls for marketing campaigns. Your team successfully represents your brand to your market. You have strong management in place and can easily report on key statistics: contacts per hour, stats by rep, etc. You set goals and hit them consistently.	You have a vendor or in-house team and their performance is average. If they're in-house, you have some statistics, but not enough, and there's a fair amount of turnover on the team. In fact, you're always training someone new. You see the value in using telemarketing and you think your operation could improve.	You don't have a telemarketing operation. Sales reps make their own cold-calls but they simply don't make enough. When prospects call from your website, there frequently isn't a person available to talk with them live. And when you need to include a phone call in a marketing campaign, it's an enormous battle to get reps to make calls.

How Telemarketing Aligns with Strategy

Campaigns using telemarketing should support your positioning and brand strategy. Most of this is conveyed through each individual telemarketer, so write your scripts and train your reps to adhere to the personality traits of your brand.

Key Concepts & Steps

Set your goals

You can use telemarketing in many ways; brainstorm the campaigns that will work best for your company. For example, you may need to generate leads for your sales team or use telemarketing to support other marketing campaigns.

DOWNLOAD hundreds of plans for these marketing activities at www.MarketingMO.com.

marketing MO

SHARE this ebook:

69

Forecast and budget; determine whether to build in-house or outsource

› Estimate your call volume, and then think about hours of operation, fluctuations in call volume, and the skill set you'll need in your reps.

› Your call volume also drives your headcount, software, phone system and the office space you'll need.

› These requirements will help you decide whether to use a vendor or hire and manage a team in-house. If you reach out to vendors, having these requirements ready will make your discussions easier and faster.

› Budget for everything including headcount, software licenses, bonuses and management.

Develop good scripts

Reps will need to capture attention, build value, and close; a good script will help them do it consistently.

› Make your scripts conversational, simple, and focused on the end goal.

› It helps to make and listen to calls as you're developing and refining your script. What looks good on paper may not work on the phone.

› Get feedback from your team as well.

Train and coach your team

Regular coaching and quality assurance is crucial.

› Engage your reps, role-play and guide them through calls.

› Listen to calls regularly, evaluate your reps and coach them to improve their performance.

Report your results

› Define the reports that you'll need—your system may not be able to provide all of the data, but you can probably find an alternate solution.

› Use reports to consistently evaluate progress and improve your campaigns.

Next Steps

As you design and manage telemarketing campaigns, evaluate the effectiveness of the tools used in the campaign, and focus on continually improving your tactical execution.

Once your campaign is running, it's all about execution, so manage your team and devote the resources necessary for success.

SHARE
this ebook:

Trade Shows & Events

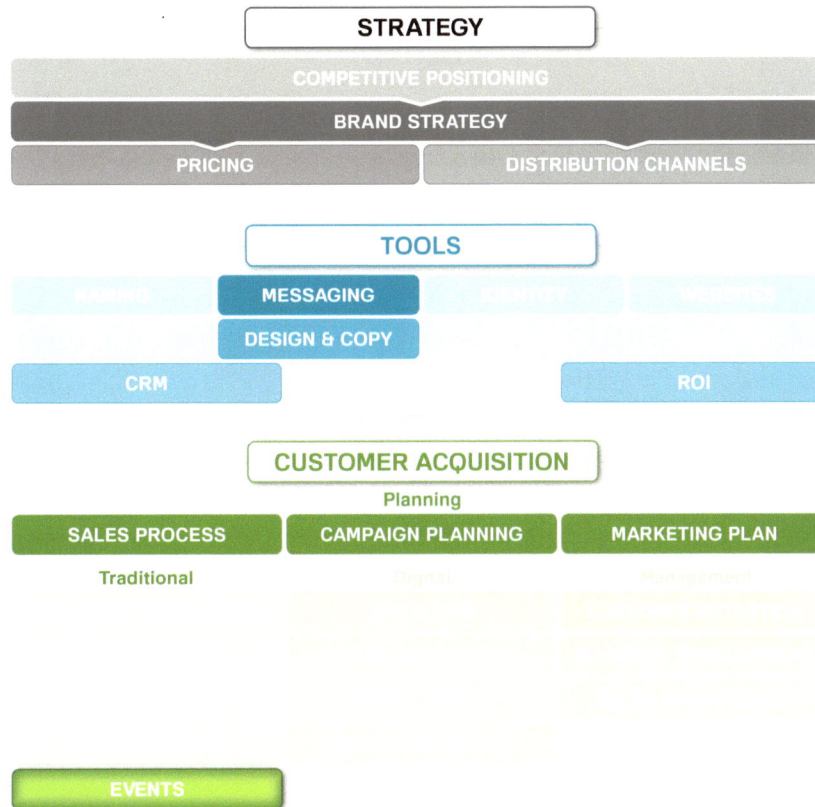

STRATEGY

COMPETITIVE POSITIONING

BRAND STRATEGY

PRICING · DISTRIBUTION CHANNELS

TOOLS

MESSAGING

DESIGN & COPY

CRM · ROI

CUSTOMER ACQUISITION

Planning

SALES PROCESS · CAMPAIGN PLANNING · MARKETING PLAN

Traditional

EVENTS

There's an old saying in business that "people buy from people." If that's the case, it's a good idea to get people to-gether as often as possible!

Trade shows and events are gatherings for people with common interests to achieve a goal. B2B and B2C companies use them to generate leads, nurture prospects, build brand awareness, conduct training, or enhance relationships with existing partners and customers. Options include:

> **Trade shows:** You can have an exhibit booth, sponsor roundtable discussions or speeches, arrange for one of your executives give a presentation or sit on a panel, advertise in show publications and/or host your own reception.

> **Seminars or conferences:** Sponsor an industry conference or create a seminar and market it to your prospects.

> **Networking meetings:** Participate in and/or sponsor industry or local meetings; you can also create a one-time or ongoing breakfast or lunch meeting series for your prospects to attend.

> **Webinars:** Webinars are online seminars with slides and audio; you can use them to generate leads and communicate with large groups at a lower cost than a live meeting.

> **Events for the arts, sports or charities:** You can participate in these events as a sponsor with advertising, blocks of tickets, promotions and a reception for your VIPs.

DOWNLOAD hundreds of plans for these marketing activities at www.MarketingMO.com.

marketing MO

SHARE this ebook:

71

Many shows and events are major investments with numerous logistics:

> Event planning   > Promotion

> Travel   > Sales materials

> Shipping   > Sales follow-up

> Set-up   > Measurement

> Exhibit booth design and materials

When executed properly, a great event could produce a large percentage of the leads that a company needs to generate over an entire year. With a halfhearted strategy, companies usually get lackluster results.

Do you see your company in any of these scenarios?

Best Case	Neutral Case	Worst Case
You use trade shows, special events and/or webinars to generate new prospects and reach out to existing prospects and customers. You stand out from your competitors, deliver compelling information and create meaningful dialog with your market. You set goals and measure them, and you know your ROI validates the investment. You also implement marketing programs and continue dialog after the event so that leads don't fall through the cracks.	You regularly attend trade shows and you've tried a few webinars with mixed results—there's a lot of competition for your prospects' attention. At shows, your team does a decent job of qualifying leads and following up; you know that you generate new business but you don't know how much. It seems like you could be generating a lot more business from these programs, but you're not sure how to do it.	You exhibit at trade shows and you're never satisfied with your results. It's hard to stand around for days and you know that leads fall through the cracks in the weeks afterward. Your competitors are always doing something big at the shows but you haven't been able to afford anything but your booth. You haven't tried any other events because they're an enormous effort for very little payoff. You've never really been able to measure the results from the shows that you attend—you get a handful of leads and that seems to be it.

With a solid strategy, plan, investment and measurement, events can be an exciting marketing medium for B2B or B2C marketers.

How Trade Shows and Events Align with Strategy

Your events and presence at trade shows should support your positioning and brand strategy. For events, your location, theme, visuals, host or MC, refreshments, and entertainment or giveaways all work together to create an impression of your brand. For trade shows, it's your booth, materials, giveaways, and people that create the impression.

Key Concepts & Steps

Choose an event that matches your need

> Define your marketing objectives: generate leads, nurture existing leads, build relationships, train and educate, or raise visibility/brand awareness.

> Focus on the types of events that will help you meet your goals: industry events and shows, networking events, seminars and conferences, sponsored events, charity events, webinars and more.

> Brainstorm to create a list of events and themes that will fit with your goals.

SHARE
this ebook:

Outline your event strategy

Understand what your prospects need and how you can deliver it during the event. For example, think about the content that your prospects want and how you should structure the event.

Create your event plan

> Once you have a strategy, start the planning process: time, date, location, theme, event flow, materials, script, responsibilities and more.

> Plan for sales-related activities: what happens with new leads, how you'll prioritize leads, follow-up timing, materials they should receive, etc.

Promote your event

> To drive attendance or participation, develop a thorough promotional campaign with a strong call-to-action.

> Use multiple media to touch your market frequently and consistently.

> If you're sponsoring another company's event, be sure to promote your participation—don't leave it up to someone else to drive your traffic.

Script your event and execute

A good event script and plan will help you execute without problems. Create a detailed timeline; rehearse appropriate activities with your team; make sure everyone clearly understands their responsibilities.

Measure your event's success

> Review your goals-to-actual measurements and share the results with your team.

> Document everything you learned so you can use that information next time.

Next Steps

Trade shows and events typically generate new relationships or foster existing ones. It's important to set solid follow-up procedures with your team so that valuable leads don't fall through the cracks.

As you design and manage events and attend trade shows, evaluate the effectiveness of your strategy and focus on continually improving your tactical execution.

SEO and SEM

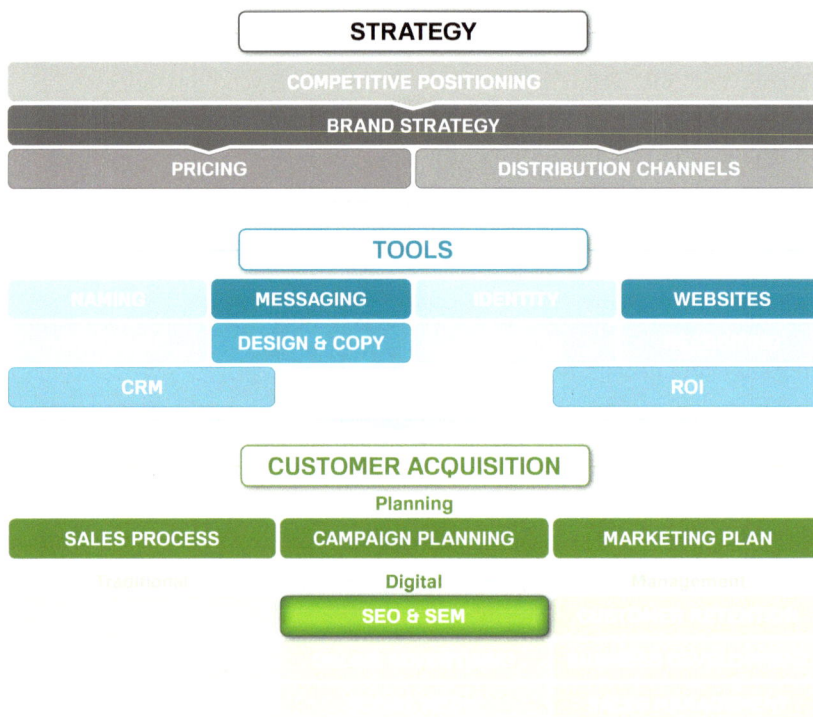

STRATEGY

COMPETITIVE POSITIONING	
BRAND STRATEGY	
PRICING	DISTRIBUTION CHANNELS

TOOLS

NAMING	MESSAGING	IDENTITY	WEBSITES
	DESIGN & COPY		
CRM			ROI

CUSTOMER ACQUISITION

Planning

SALES PROCESS	CAMPAIGN PLANNING	MARKETING PLAN

Digital

SEO & SEM

Search marketing is about gaining visibility on search engines when users search for terms that relate to your business. For most companies, ranking high in the search results isn't luck—it's a result of solid effort in one or both categories of search marketing:

Organic search (SEO): When you enter a keyword or phrase into a search engine like Google or Bing, the organic results are displayed in the main body of the page.

When your market searches for information about your products and services, you want to rank highly in search engine results. By optimizing your site, you can improve your ranking for important search terms and phrases (keywords). You can also improve your rank by getting other important sites to link to yours.

Paid search (SEM): Paid search enables you to buy listings in the "sponsored" area of a search engine. There are a variety of paid search programs, but the most common is called pay-per-click (PPC), meaning you only pay for a listing when a prospect clicks your ad.

In search marketing, companies focus on driving more traffic to targeted areas of their website. They use search to:

› Generate new leads
› Sell products
› Build their brand
› Divert traffic from their competitors

Studies show that most people—both business people and consumers considering large purchases—research their problems, potential purchases and vendors online and use a search engine in the process. And the higher the price of the product/service, the earlier in the research process they use a search engine.

For many B2B companies, generating only a handful of additional serious prospects can make a substantial difference in revenue. Using search marketing may efficiently produce these additional prospects.

Best Case	Neutral Case	Worst Case
You're generating very targeted prospects through your search marketing programs. Your site is optimized and you've built a lot of important incoming links, so you rank well in organic results for targeted keywords. You use paid search to supplement that traffic and you create custom landing pages for your campaigns to convert visitors into prospects or sales.	You've built a new website and it's been optimized for search, but you don't rank in the top 10 for any keywords other than your company name. You've tried some paid search with good success; your conversion rates on the traffic are okay but could be better. You know that search marketing is a solid opportunity—you're just figuring out how to improve your results.	Your website isn't optimized for search and you're nowhere to be found on search engines, even for very targeted terms. In fact, you may not even rank for searches on your company name. Unfortunately, your competitors show up on the first and second pages for the terms your prospects use. As a result, your competitors are winning new business and furthering their lead in the market.

How Search Engine Marketing Aligns with Strategy

Campaigns using search engines should support your positioning and brand strategy, contributing to the experience that you wish to deliver and the mindshare that you wish to own. This includes your ad copy, landing pages, and page descriptions that appear in organic results.

Key Concepts & Steps

Create your search strategy

Review your short- and long-term goals to help determine whether to focus on organic or paid search (or both). It takes time to improve your organic search rankings, but you can launch a paid search campaign today. However, there are other considerations: the amount of traffic that you need, your budget, and your marketing objectives. Once you've reviewed the pros and cons of each, you can select the search strategy that's right for you.

Generate a list of keywords

Before you can optimize your site or launch a paid campaign, generate a list of keywords—terms your prospects use when looking for information that you can deliver. You can brainstorm, copy keywords from competitors, or use online tools (such as Google's Keyword Tool) to generate a list and estimate traffic.

Optimize your website

› Rewrite your content and code your pages so that they're optimized for search engines.
› Make sure the content is organized in the best possible manner.
› Eliminate any technologies that prevent search engines from reading your content (for example, search engines can't read graphics or Flash content).

- › Register your site in important directories that play a vital role in search engine results.
- › If you don't have anyone on staff that is an SEO expert, hire an outside specialist.

Generate inbound links

Search engines reward you when sites link to yours—they assume that your site must be valuable and you'll rank higher in search results. The higher the "page rank" of the sites that link to you, the more they help to raise your own ranking. You want links from popular industry authorities, recognized directories, and reputable companies and organizations.

Implement additional Internet campaigns

These programs can improve your search results:

- › Using social media, online advertising and online PR to generate traffic and links
- › Including a blog on your site
- › Distributing search-optimized press releases on the web
- › Creating RSS feeds to distribute updated content from your site to other websites

Start testing paid search

To begin using paid search, you'll:

- › Develop targeted landing pages for each campaign
- › Write your ad(s)
- › Create an account with a search network
- › Set up your campaign with the network
- › Set a daily or monthly budget
- › Start tracking your results

Next Steps

As you design and manage campaigns using search engines, evaluate the effectiveness of the tools used in the campaign, and focus on continually improving your tactical execution.

Pay close attention to click-through rates and conversion rates; for most paid search campaigns, the difference between positive and negative ROI is thorough testing and detailed management.

Online Advertising

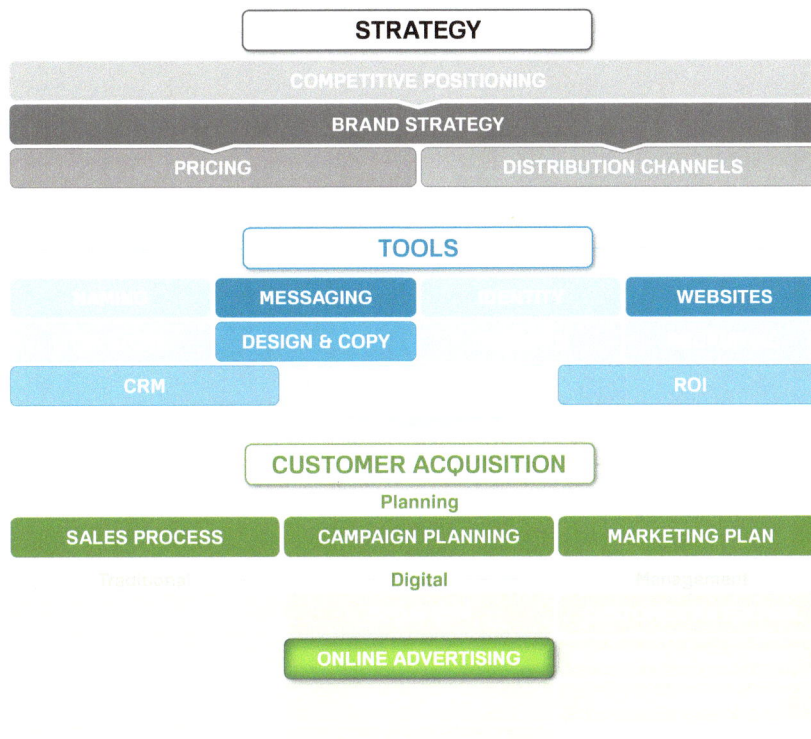

Internet marketing isn't just for consumer marketers or large B2B firms—it's a powerful vehicle for companies of all sizes.

Online advertising offers marketers an opportunity to reach very broad or very targeted prospects to generate leads, communicate a message and raise visibility. The term refers to three general types of campaigns:

› Banner ads placed on other websites

› Ads or sponsored content on targeted email newsletters

› Affiliate programs that enable you to put your ad on another company's website and in return you pay a commission on clicks or sales

While a B2B marketer has a smaller universe of prospects than a consumer marketer, the value of each prospect is typically far greater. With a targeted campaign and a good offer, you may only need to generate a handful of highly qualified prospects to produce substantial revenue.

Here are three examples of online ad campaigns:

Generate New Leads	Direct Sales	Increase Your Visibility
Promote a white paper, webinar or demo that can help prospects who are in the early phases of their research. Drive them to a special landing page where you provide details about the offer and capture key pieces of data so you can follow up when the prospect is ready.	Run ads to sell a particular product or service. Drive prospects to a special landing page that describes your offer in detail. You create supplemental pages to provide additional information if needed. You focus on converting those prospects into sales.	Run a campaign to share a message, promote an event or offer, or raise awareness about your products. Your goal is twofold: Drive click-throughs and generate awareness. You use landing pages designed to convert a visitor into a prospect or customer.

What are the benefits of online advertising?

> **Timing:** Reach people when they're actively looking for information and solutions.

> **Immediacy:** You can test and launch very quickly and generate response almost immediately.

> **Targeting:** You can deliver your message to very specific audiences.

> **Lead generation and nurturing:** You can capture prospects early, provide valuable information, and nurture them throughout the sales process.

> **Cost:** You can reach a large audience quickly and at a lower cost than many other types of media.

> **Scalability:** You can run campaigns of any size, at any budget level.

As with any marketing program, it's important to develop a good strategy, target your audience, test, measure and improve—especially because it's easy and inexpensive to test different aspects of your campaigns in order to generate the best possible results.

Best Case	Neutral Case	Worst Case
Your online ad campaigns are a strong element in your marketing mix. You use them to generate prospects and customers, but gaining visibility is also important. You calculate ROI so you can compare the return of these investments compared to your other programs. You continually test your ads and landing pages to maximize your response rates.	You run campaigns periodically and they're moderately successful. Prices are high, but you reach a targeted audience. You occasionally test and tweak your ads, but it isn't a priority. Since you use cost per click to measure success, you can't accurately calculate ROI, but you're satisfied with what you're paying for traffic. You think you can generate even more traffic, but without better metrics, you can't divert more funds to these campaigns.	You've advertised on a few sites and generated some traffic, but you don't have data to indicate whether your campaigns are successful beyond initial visits. You don't create special landing pages—you drive visitors to your home page, and you rarely test your ads. You cringe at the prices for the sites you'd really like to use, and you think you're wasting money since you're paying for impressions not clicks.

How Online Advertising Aligns with Strategy

Campaigns using online media should support your positioning and brand strategy, contributing to the experience that you wish to deliver and the mindshare that you wish to own.

This includes your ad graphics, copy, as well as your landing pages and conversion process.

SHARE
this ebook:

Key Concepts & Steps

Before you launch an online campaign, it's important to have a good website that can measure your traffic and convert visitors to prospects or customers. It's also helpful to address your online campaigns in your annual marketing plan and budget.

Develop a tangible goal

For example, determine how many click-throughs or leads that you need to generate, and then estimate your response rates to figure out how many impressions you'll need. Make sure that you know how you'll measure your campaign as well.

Target your audience

Profile and target your audience. You can reach a large audience with your ad, but that doesn't mean you should—narrow targeting means you can speak more directly to the needs of your target market.

Create a good offer and compelling call-to-action

Your ad needs to generate interest and get people to click through to your website to learn more—give them a reason, a benefit. Keep your message simple and clear.

Focus on conversion

When you run a great ad, continue the message and momentum on your website. Don't drive prospects to your home page—instead, create unique landing pages that focus on the topic you used to generate their interest. Focus and sell!

Test your ad variables

It's easy and inexpensive to test your online campaigns. You can test the offer, the design of your ad, the size and location of the ad, or the sites that you choose. Start with the element that's most important—for example, the offer—and create two versions of the ad. Then run them against each other to see which one performs best.

Next Steps

As you design and manage campaigns using online media, evaluate the effectiveness of the tools used in the campaign, and focus on continually improving your tactical execution.

Keep refining your online campaigns and your website to drive and convert traffic.

Social Media

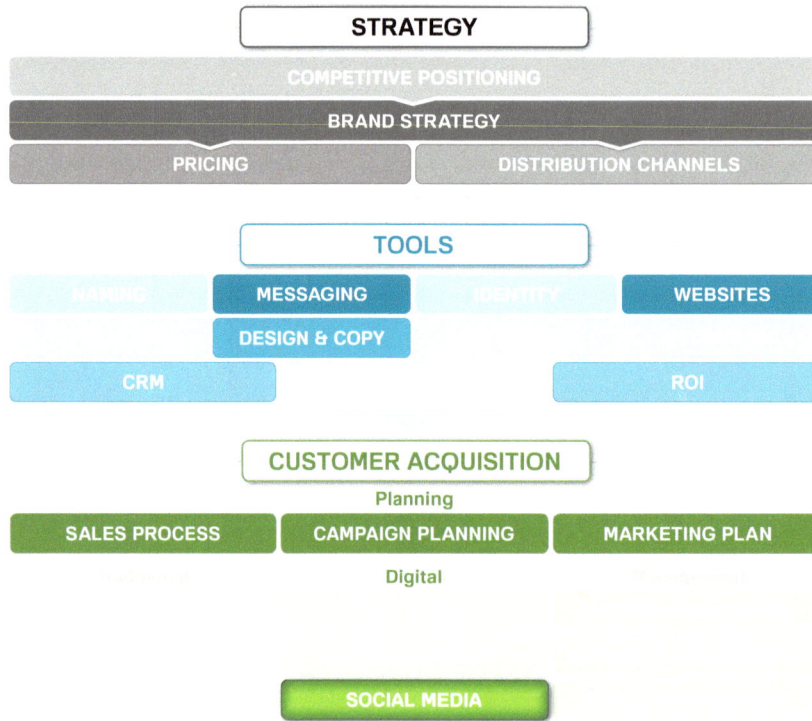

By now, everyone is probably familiar with social media. But how many marketers truly understand how to use social media to achieve business goals?

Social media describes the category of websites that allow people to connect, communicate and share information in real time on the Internet. Social media allows almost anyone to be a publisher—to disseminate information quickly without controls.

Social media has become a powerful tool that marketers can use to:

> Build brand awareness
> Interact directly with customers and the market
> Launch promotions
> Distribute news
> Generate leads
> Monitor competitors
> Build links
> Connect with thought-leaders
> Find out how the market perceives you
> Establish thought-leadership
> Gather market research
> Facilitate sales

Social media evolved from the "Web 2.0" technologies in the early 2000s—blogging platforms and wikis. The number of social media websites—or from a marketers' perspective, social media tools—is immense. From 2006 to 2012, it was estimated that there were over 300 popular social media websites. There are probably thousands of others, and over 100,000,000 blogs.

Since most social media websites are free, it's easy to "go social" and start interacting with others. There are substantial costs to make it effective, however, such as graphic design, content development, publishing and account management, listening to the conversation, responding to feedback and monitoring and managing performance.

Social media works well for certain types of business goals, but not so well for others. Since the barriers to start are so low, many marketers begin using social media without a carefully crafted plan and without the proper commitment, which typically leads to wasted time and a lost investment. Worse yet, the crowd can be a harsh critic and negative information moves through the Web instantaneously, punishing bad social campaigns or a company's negative behavior.

The good news is that most social media sites fall into a handful of different categories:

› **Social Bookmarking:** Interaction by tagging websites and searching through websites bookmarked by other people.

› **Social News & Voting:** Interaction by voting for shared articles and content and commenting on them.

› **Social Content:** Blogs, micro blogs (Twitter), wikis, presentations, documents, photo and video sharing. Interact by sharing information and commenting on user submissions.

› **Social Networking:** Interaction by adding friends, commenting on profiles, joining groups and having discussions. A number of these sites include features from the other categories.

If you're just starting with social media, thinking about the categories instead of all the individual sites (Facebook, Twitter, Slideshare, LinkedIn, Tumblr, etc.) makes it easier to understand how to use them to achieve your business goals.

Best Case	Neutral Case	Worst Case
Social media isn't just a promotional channel for Julie's Chocolates; it's a way to interact with their customers and enhance their brand. Julie's marketing director commits 25% of her marketing budget to social media. She uses Facebook to launch promotions and gain customer feedback, Twitter to interact with fans and promote sales, and YouTube and Vimeo to distribute humorous videos about how the team comes up with ideas for new candy shapes. Social media plays an integral role in Julie's brand strategy. It adds personality to the brand and connects it directly to their market.	Encompass Healthcare is a large, multi-state healthcare agency. They have a substantial marketing budget, focusing mostly on traditional media such as print, radio and television. The company has created a Facebook page and regularly tweets on Twitter, but the content is generally a rehash of the ads and promotions from their traditional media campaigns. The marketing team knows they should have a social media presence, but no one is dedicated to using social media to interact with the market and bring their brand directly to members; they simply view it as another place to promote themselves.	Digital Training & Distribution creates and delivers industry-specific training videos for a variety of technical products. The company uses its sales reps as the primary delivery channel for information about what's happening in the industry. And, the sales reps handle the marketing function, generating new leads and turning prospects into customers on a one-to-one basis. Years ago, the company launched a quarterly newsletter and, while their market appreciated the information, the company didn't make a concerted effort to keep it alive. Since the company focuses little effort on marketing, it has no interest in dedicating time and resources to interacting with its market using social media.

As you're considering how you might use social media, here's a helpful tip: think of social media as a cocktail party . . . online. You can mingle and share information and participate in a global conversation. But remember that once you publish something socially, whether it's a comment or piece of content, you've lost control of it and it can be indexed by the search engines, sometimes forever.

Since you have no control over how the crowd speaks about your company or brand, an unhappy customer can generate quite a buzz. An example is United Airlines, who damaged a customer's guitar and refused to replace it, spawning the hit YouTube song United Breaks Guitars, decrying United's customer service and brand.

How Social Media Aligns with Strategy

Campaigns using social should support your positioning and brand strategy, contributing to the experience that you wish to deliver and the mindshare that you wish to own.

This includes the graphic design of your social media sites, but more importantly, it's influenced by the communication from your people—the responses, tone, and messages that they convey.

Key Concepts and Steps

Most social media campaigns use multiple social media websites and are tied into your own website. Make sure that your site is updated and can handle social media success (i.e. a lot of traffic) if you achieve it. And make sure that it reflects your brand.

Develop your campaign around specific business goals

Don't go social just because everyone else is. Determine your specific business goals and decide if social media can help you accomplish them.

Research and listen

Since social media is a conversation, the first step before planning any campaign is to take the time to listen to the conversation. See what's happening on numerous sites, identify the influencers and think about the conversation:

› Should you participate?

› How can you participate and add value?

› Will participating help you achieve your business goals?

Create a social media plan

Few campaigns will be successful without a plan, and it's just as important with social media. Carefully target your audience, determine the message you desire to communicate, secure the creative and technical resources you need, and plan the time on your calendar to execute.

Invest in quality content

Most social media campaigns involve content, whether it's commentary, excerpts, thoughts, presentations, pictures or video. The Web is cluttered, so distribute the highest-quality content possible.

SHARE
this ebook:

Commit the time to manage and interact

While some social media campaigns become instant hits, they're the exception, not the norm. B2C marketers can typically create more interesting campaigns that garner immediate feedback. Most B2B marketers find that the nature of their content requires more hard work to distribute and generate conversation. Many successful B2B campaigns have taken months of laborious work, day-in and day-out, to build a following and generate buzz.

Be respectful and follow best practices

Online conversation moves quickly, and sometimes feedback can be harsh. It's a good idea to avoid negativity, and be respectful of others, especially your critics. Be transparent, admit mistakes, and handle your online conversations with great care—you never know how they can influence public perception about you or your brand.

Measure and refine

Whether you're measuring specific metrics like number of followers, links, group interactions or web traffic, or a return on your social media investment, review your data to see how you're progressing and what adjustments you might need to make. This will help you see if one element of your campaign is working better than another, enabling you to shift resources there for better performance.

Next Steps

As you design and manage campaigns using social media, evaluate the effectiveness of the tools used in the campaign, and focus on continually improving your tactical execution.

Social media has evolved faster than almost any other medium in history. What's hot today isn't always popular tomorrow. Remember Friendster? There's no guarantee Facebook and Twitter will stay on top . . . keep up-to-date on the trends.

Email Marketing

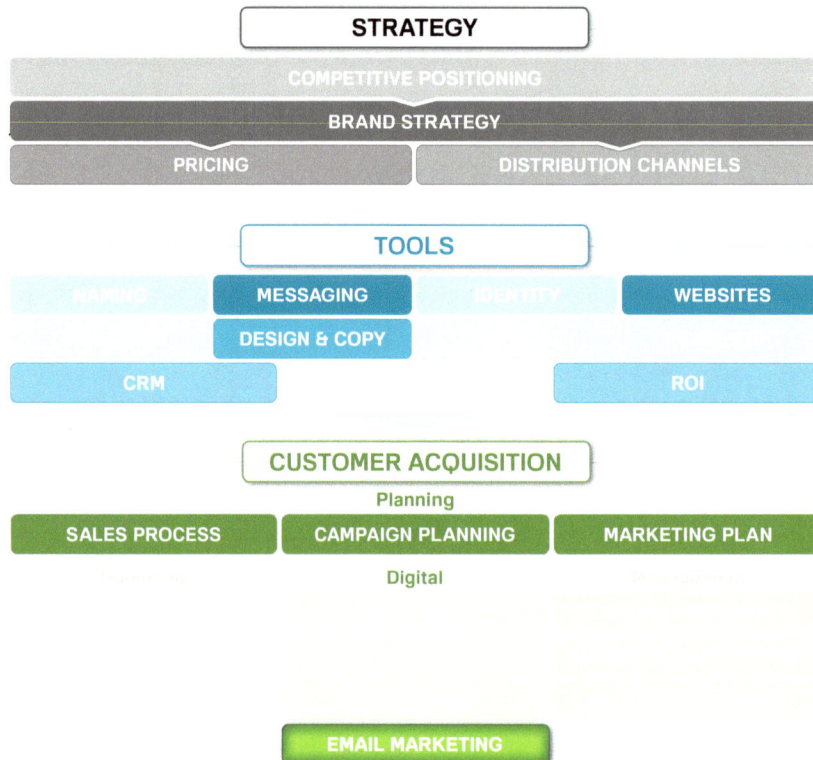

STRATEGY

COMPETITIVE POSITIONING

BRAND STRATEGY

PRICING

DISTRIBUTION CHANNELS

TOOLS

NAMING

MESSAGING

IDENTITY

WEBSITES

DESIGN & COPY

CRM

ROI

CUSTOMER ACQUISITION

Planning

SALES PROCESS

CAMPAIGN PLANNING

MARKETING PLAN

Digital

EMAIL MARKETING

Email marketing has been a staple for consumer marketers since the mid-1990s. A few years later, B2B marketers discovered its value, and email campaigns have become an important tool for businesses in all stages and industries.

Email marketing enables you to cost-effectively communicate with your market in a way that's immediate and relevant. With email, you can:

› Nurture leads

› Build brand awareness

› Obtain prospects

› Build customer loyalty

› Generate sales

You can usually launch a campaign and measure your results quickly, making email a great option for time-sensitive programs. It's easy and inexpensive to test different aspects of your campaign on a segment of your list, so you can hone your creative and your offer to generate the best possible results.

SHARE
this ebook:

Here are three sample email campaigns:

Generate New Leads	Direct Sales	Build Brand Awareness
Rent a list and send a short, compelling message to generate interest in your product. Drive prospects to a special page on your website to download a white paper, a demo or other offer. Capture basic information and follow up via phone several days later.	Create a special offer for your current prospects and customers; compel them to click to your website to learn and buy.	Use email to keep in touch with prospects and customers. Deliver timely, valuable information that makes them want to read your messages. Add news about your company, special offers, etc., but focus on content and information rather than pure sales.

Email is more editorial than advertising, and it's powerful because it can support and even drive a sales process. Yet, like any medium, it has its challenges. B2C email marketing to cold lists has a terrible response rate. Social media is reducing people's reliance on email. Businesspeople often still receive hundreds of emails (or more) each day, so B2B marketers need to get past spam filters and give people a reason to read. You'll also need a strong offer, valuable editorial content, appropriate design and a good fulfillment and measurement process.

While you can reach a wide audience with email, that doesn't mean you should. It's most effective when you really target so you can speak to specific needs. Think of it as a one-to-one communication—personalized, relevant and timely—not a blast.

If you've used email in the past, do you see your company in one of these scenarios?

Best Case	Neutral Case	Worst Case
You have a strong email program with very specific goals. You use technology to deliver your messages effectively. Your campaigns offer strong content and messages; you create custom landing pages to convert clicks to prospects. You continually test your designs, copy, list and offer to improve your response. As a result, you usually meet your ROI and business goals.	You perform some email marketing and are generally satisfied with the results. You send announcements about products and offers; you occasionally use email to generate leads or keep your name in front of existing ones. You occasionally test a campaign before launch, but it isn't a major priority. You know that your campaigns could be stronger, but you haven't had time to improve them.	You use email as a quick-fix—when you're low on leads, you do a blast message; if you haven't reached out to customers in a while, you create a quick newsletter. You generally don't target your prospects—you blast one message to your entire list. You don't test your campaigns, and you don't know how many of your messages are actually delivered.

How Email Marketing Aligns with Strategy

Campaigns using email should support your positioning and brand strategy, contributing to the experience that you wish to deliver and the mindshare that you wish to own. This includes your email design, copy, delivery frequency, CAN-SPAM compliance and opt-out procedure.

Key Concepts & Steps

Use email to meet the goals you set in your annual marketing plan; you can also use them as part of a broader marketing campaign. You'll also need to make sure your website is strong enough to support your campaign.

Develop your campaign around specific goals

Take the time to strategize and plan your campaign:

› Develop a tangible objective—for example, to generate a specific number of leads, demo requests, meetings, or purchases.

› Profile and target your audience.

› Create a good offer and compelling call-to-action, and present it early in your message—readers skim.

› Plan a series of emails to create an ongoing campaign—it takes multiple touches to generate response.

› Don't forget fulfillment—if your prospects expect a phone call or email, deliver it quickly or you could lose their interest.

Invest in good content

You probably don't want all of your emails to focus on product or service promotions. Readers will tire of them. Instead, offer information that's relevant to your recipients. It's an investment to develop that content, but it's the content that gets people to open your messages and continue to read them over time.

Choose the right technology

If you've never launched an email campaign, you'll probably need to use an email service provider (ESP), typically a web-based service. Choose a reputable ESP to help you stay compliant with spam legislation and get your messages to your prospects' inboxes—a major challenge in email marketing. A good ESP can raise your delivery rate, manage your opt-in and opt-out process, keep your email list clean and provide reports that can help you improve your results.

Be respectful and follow industry practices

Make sure that you're following accepted industry practices—you'll improve your probability of success.

› Mail to your house list regularly—even corporate emails change rapidly. The more time between campaigns, the higher your rate of bad addresses—and those "bounces" could trigger spam alerts.

› Make sure your recipients can easily opt-out of future communications.

› If you're buying or renting a list, make sure it's an "opt-in" list.

Continually test, refine and improve

It's always wise to test before launching a campaign. If you're working with a new ESP or list, evaluate your delivery and response rate before you roll out. Keep testing and improving your subject lines, headlines and copy, design, offer, landing pages, even the delivery timing. You'll improve all your campaigns in the process.

Next Steps

As your use of email increases, keep learning about open rates, subject lines, list fatigue, and other ways to improve your campaigns.

SHARE
this ebook:

Customer Retention

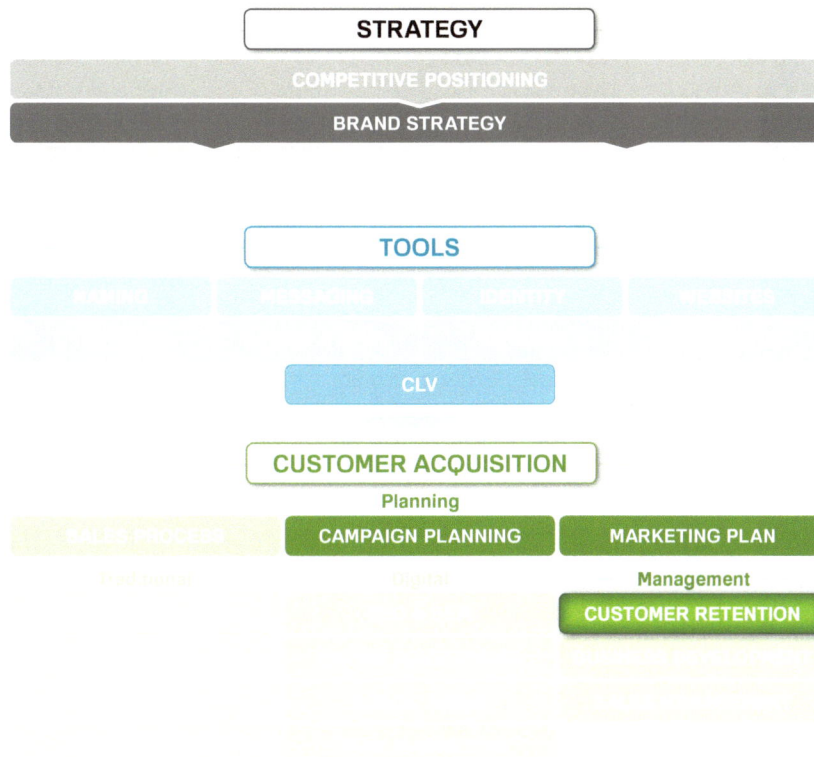

How much have you invested in your marketing programs over the last few years? Thousands? Tens of thousands? Millions? Tens of millions?

Customer retention is about keeping the customers that you already spent money to acquire. And if you're in an industry where your customers make multiple purchases over the years, your entire team should be very focused on retaining those customers by:

> Delivering service that's consistent with your brand

> Cross-selling, up-selling and asking for referrals from existing customers

> Developing programs to increase customer loyalty and decrease turnover

> Knowing the lifetime value for different segments and using that data to improve your marketing

> Prioritizing retention as a major focus in your annual marketing plan

Studies show that it costs ten times more to generate a new customer than to maintain an existing one. If you have a small number of customers, losing a few could cripple your company. Even if you have a large number of customers, a small increase in your retention rate should dramatically increase your profits.

In his book The Loyalty Effect, Fred Reichheld writes that "a 5% improvement in customer retention rates will yield between a 25% to 100% increase in profits across a wide range of industries."

With strong retention marketing, it's much easier to grow your revenue and profitability. Do you see your company in any of these scenarios?

Best Case	Neutral Case	Worst Case
Your company is focused on customer retention and it has paid off. Renewals are high; you put a lot of effort into campaigns and service for existing customers. Incentives encourage sales and support reps to keep customers happy, and you use financial modeling and surveys to identify problems and focus on vulnerable customers. Your revenue has grown substantially each year because you're adding new customers without losing current ones.	You know how important it is to retain customers. The reps who service existing customers are good, but you've lost some customers that you shouldn't have. You've sent out some surveys but haven't done much with the data from them. And you struggle with the commission on sales to existing customers—some people argue that you shouldn't pay at all because they're house accounts. As a result, you have to replace numerous current customers each year.	You don't formally market to your current customers. You know that your service could be better, but you haven't had the time to develop an improvement plan. You definitely have more turnover than you'd like. As a result, you're continually investing to generate new customers. Your revenue and profit margins are much lower than they could be, and the churning takes its toll on your organization.

How Customer Retention Aligns with Strategy

Customer service, retention activities and campaigns to existing customers should support your positioning and brand strategy, contributing to the experience that you wish to deliver and the mindshare that you wish to own.

You can work on your customer retention strategy at any time, and marketing campaigns to them may be an important part of your strategy. You may also decide to increase your focus on retention when you're writing your annual marketing plan. But if you're losing customers, don't hesitate to focus your energy on retention right now.

Key Concepts & Steps

Determine your retention strategy

Your positioning and brand strategy should drive your retention plan. For example, if your method for delivering value is customer intimacy, your customers are expecting great customer service. If they're buying on price, you'll usually focus more on automating service to minimize costs.

Build your team

In some B2B industries, the original sales rep is the best person to manage an existing client—for example, the account may require ongoing selling. In other cases, it's better to transition the customer to an account rep who focuses on day-to-day management.

Once you've decided how to structure the team, determine how many people that you'll need and start recruiting.

Pay commission for renewals and growing the business

Your current customers are your most valuable asset—if your sales reps don't earn commission on renewals, they'll have more incentive to spend their time chasing new business instead.

Market to existing customers

Put as much effort into your current customer campaigns as you put into the rest of your marketing programs. Know your audience, grab their attention, focus on the offer, measure your results. Use campaigns to:

> Nurture your customer relationships

> Encourage customers to buy again

> Expand your relationships by cross-selling, up-selling and asking for referrals

> Identify customers who are at risk of defecting

> Continually deliver on your brand promise

Measure purchase intent and loyalty, not "satisfaction"

Customer feedback can help you improve your products and enhance your relationship with your customers. However, it's not effective to measure "customer satisfaction" because it's so vague. "Satisfied" doesn't mean they intend to keep buying. Instead, focus on behavior: Ask whether they intend to buy again and why or why not. Ask what three things you can improve upon and whether they'll provide referrals. These questions provide more actionable insight than "satisfaction."

Use data to evaluate large groups of customers

If you don't have personal relationships with your customers, use data to identify customers who haven't purchased in the normal timeframe. They may be at risk of defecting and you can launch retention campaigns and encourage them to stay.

Next Steps

Refine and improve your customer retention strategy and execution—it may deliver the highest ROI of all of your marketing programs.

Service and manage your customer base, evaluate the effectiveness of the tools used, and focus on continually improving your tactical execution.

Business Development

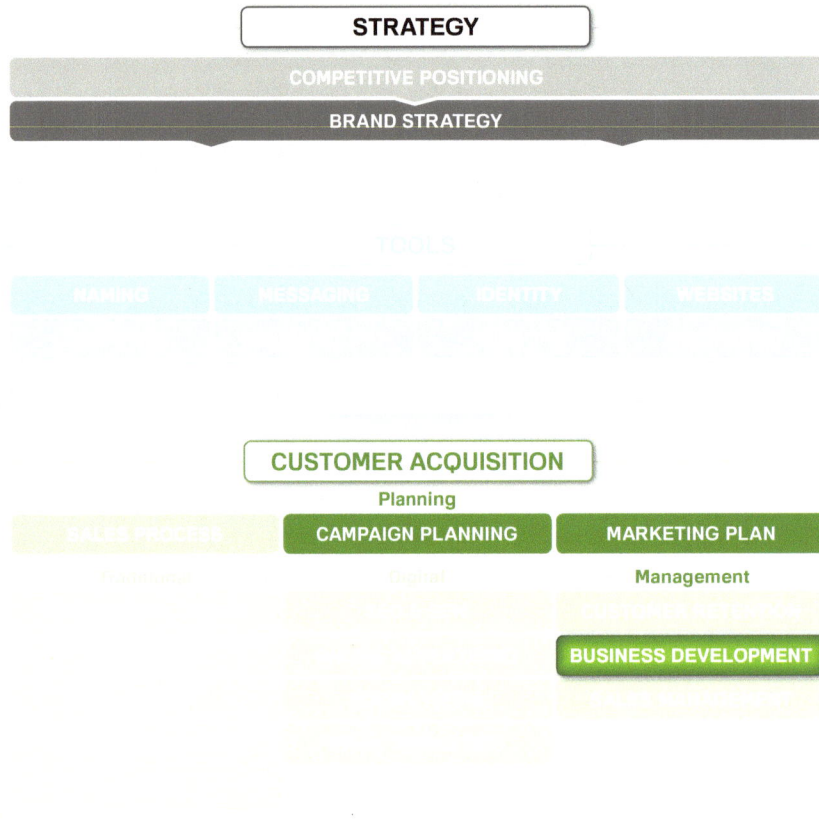

STRATEGY

COMPETITIVE POSITIONING

BRAND STRATEGY

TOOLS

| NAMING | MESSAGING | IDENTITY | WEBSITES |

CUSTOMER ACQUISITION

Planning

| CAMPAIGN PLANNING | MARKETING PLAN |

Management

| BUSINESS DEVELOPMENT |

Organizations apply the term "business development" (a.k.a. "biz dev") to a variety of activities.

In this section, "business development" refers to high-level partnerships that generate revenue, create better products and/or increase efficiency. These partnerships can help you:

› Access new markets

› Increase sales to existing markets

› Improve your access to technology

› Boost your productivity

› Gain capital (human or financial)

In a true partnership, companies collaborate to achieve a common goal. It's more than a short-term promotion, such as a special offer or marketing to each other's customers. Instead, it's an agreement to do business together while sharing responsibilities, resources, risks and rewards.

Here are three examples of true partnerships:

To Create New Products	To Increase Efficiency	To Create New Services
A computer manufacturer enters a partnership with a fashion designer to create a limited-edition laptop and matching case. They create a team of employees from both companies to design and market the product. The computer manufacturer produces the computers, the designer creates the bag, and they share revenue fairly based on their contributions and cost structure.	A software company has a fantastic new product but is inundated with customer service calls that they can't handle. They approach a telemarketing firm that specializes in the software industry. Instead of just hiring the telemarketing firm, they create a partnership. The telemarketing firm provides service for a greatly reduced fee, then receives a substantial commission for selling the software company's other related software. The partners work closely together to maximize their revenue on the sales program.	A design firm partners with a direct mail fulfillment firm to offer each other's services to their respective clients. Each company promotes the partnership to new prospects and existing customers. They offer the service with a single point of contact—if a design client needs mail services, the design firm manages the implementation rather than just referring the client to the mail firm. Each company bills the other at special rates so there's room for a fair markup, providing each company with additional revenue.

In these examples, each company has distinct responsibilities in the partnership. They each devote resources (either time or money) to the program, and if it fails, they have similar levels of risk. They've also fairly divided the rewards.

The first step in a successful partnership is structure; the right arrangement aligns both companies toward an important common goal. The second step is execution; a partnership should be managed like any business with careful attention to detail, solid communication and focus on the end goals.

With the right structure and management, your business development deals have the greatest potential for success.

Best Case	Neutral Case	Worst Case
The partnership is balanced and productive for both parties. You share responsibilities, resources, risks and rewards, and the partnership delivers substantial revenue, cost savings or new opportunities for both companies.	Your partnership isn't balanced—perhaps you have more responsibilities and resources allocated or you don't share fairly in the rewards. It produces value, though not what you had expected; you hope that the situation will improve with time.	You enter into a partnership and invest substantial resources, but the partnership goes awry. Your "partner" isn't delivering as needed and you don't have much recourse—your partner isn't really providing resources or sharing risk. As a result, you end the partnership and lose valuable time and money on the deal.

Since these partnerships involve multiple departments in each company, there are usually a number of people involved in the deal. It's often an executive or high-level "biz dev" person leading the process for each company, although in small companies, a sales or marketing executive will typically take the reins. However, creating a partnership is more complex than pure sales—it requires a solid understanding of the business and operational objectives of multiple organizations.

How Business Development Aligns with Strategy

Partnerships that you create from your business development efforts should support your positioning and brand strategy, contributing to the experience that you wish to deliver and the mindshare that you wish to own.

Choose partnerships carefully; the wrong one can hurt your perception in the marketplace and damage your brand.

Key Concepts & Steps

Identify potential partnerships

Brainstorm to identify partnerships that can help you meet your goals. For example, there may be related companies with customer relationships in a different market; you may have vendors or suppliers who can help you improve your products or firms that can help you round out your services.

Think about structure as well—the resources that each party would provide, how the partnership would be managed and what each party would invest and earn.

Identify the right "biz dev" person to lead the project

A good "biz dev" person has a broad understanding of business strategy and operations; s/he can also negotiate and close a complex sale. It's a different skill set than many sales reps offer, but you may have a rep or executive on your team who can do these kinds of deals—or you may tackle it yourself.

Pitch a partnership

Develop a strong pitch to capture the attention of your potential partners; focus on the high-level benefits for each party. As you move through the sales process, cover all aspects of the partnership including detailed structure and terms.

Share responsibilities, resources, risks and rewards

You have a much stronger chance of success when a partnership is balanced. As you negotiate the deal, make sure that your interests are completely aligned and that each party is contributing in all areas.

Next Steps

As you set up partnerships resulting from business development activities, evaluate the effectiveness of the partnership, and focus on continually improving your tactical execution.

Make sure that your company manages and executes its responsibilities, so that you'll reap the full benefits. As part of the partnership you may launch new marketing campaigns—treat them as you would any other marketing program.

Sales Management

Improving your sales management is one of the easiest ways to increase your revenue and profitability.

Sales management is about leading the people and process your company uses to sell to prospects and convert them into customers. Responsibilities include:

- Building the right sales strategy
- Hiring the right team
- Creating the right compensation plans, territories and quotas
- Setting the right projections
- Motivating your team

- Tracking revenue against goals
- Resolving conflicts
- Training and coaching sales reps
- Managing processes
- Getting the sale!

Why are we talking about sales management in a marketing book?

- Sales and marketing serve one purpose: to generate revenue. They should be completely aligned in their understanding of customer needs, their messages, and in the process they use to identify, sell, close and manage prospects and customers. They should work together as a unit, providing valuable feedback to each other to improve all of their strategies.

- If you're B2B, your sales team is the voice of your company. In fact, your reps may be the only people with direct customer interaction. They may be responsible for prospecting, selling and managing existing customers. They control the dialogue with your market, gather feedback, and deliver much of your brand experience.

› The sales team will make or break your marketing efforts. Even if you're not personally responsible for the sales team, it's important to understand their role and draw on that knowledge to create better marketing programs.

› When departments aren't aligned, your company wastes time and opportunity. For example, when salespeople rewrite literature and tools to their liking, your messages are diluted and salespeople are doing something other than selling.

Small improvements in your team's skills and processes can often produce substantial results. Even great salespeople can benefit from coaching; if your team is struggling, there's room for improvement. And with the right attention to your pipeline and goals, you can make sure that you're on track to hit your numbers and make adjustments as needed.

Best Case	Neutral Case	Worst Case
Your sales team is a revenue-producing machine. They have the right skills and experience; they're motivated to come in each day and close business. You coach them regularly to improve their performance. When problems arise, they're dealt with swiftly. The sales team does a great job delivering the company's brand experience, messages and personality.	There are strong and weak players on the sales team. Some require a lot more hand-holding than you'd like; there isn't always time to give them the help they need. As a result, their close ratios are much lower. They're probably not hitting their quotas, but they're not a major liability to the company.	Your sales team isn't strong. You may not have a dedicated sales manager to help improve performance. They may not have enough experience, especially if you're a small company that can't yet afford the big hitters. You have a pipeline but don't know what's happening with prospects; it takes longer than it should to close deals. You suspect that you need an entirely new sales operation.

How Sales Management Aligns with Strategy

Your sales team should support your positioning and brand strategy, contributing to the experience that you wish to deliver and the mindshare that you wish to own.

This is accomplished by good hiring, training and strong management. Have your team represent the personality traits of your brand, and look to hire people that fit them well.

Key Concepts & Steps

Create the right compensation plan and tie it to your revenue goals

Great salespeople want to make money. Tie the plan to your revenue goals and make sure that you're compensating your reps for the right things. For example, if your reps don't earn commission for managing "house" accounts, they'll spend their time going after new business, and you could lose valuable existing customers.

Set realistic quotas

Be realistic about what a salesperson can accomplish in a set timeframe. Good salespeople can be demotivated by unrealistic quotas, which can lead to turnover.

Hire the right people

To build a great team, start with a strong recruiting effort. Create a detailed job description so you know exactly what you need in your candidates. Cast a wide net, use a thorough interview process, and go after the candidates you really want.

Coach and provide feedback

A good manager actively works with the sales team. Train your reps thoroughly and coach them to improve their skills. Go on calls, establish performance measurements, and provide feedback. If a rep has trouble in a particular area, create an action plan and measure improvement.

Generate good reports

You'll need good sales reports to measure team and individual progress. Yet you don't want your sales reps to spend valuable sales time creating manual lists and reports. Instead, develop automated reporting processes—for example, create reports in your CRM system. With good reports, you can identify problems early and take action quickly.

Motivate!

Good sales reps want to get better—encourage them to read, attend seminars, network, and keep refining their skills.

Next Steps

As you manage your sales team throughout the year, evaluate the effectiveness of your people, process and tools, and focus on continually improving your tactical execution.

Hire the right people, manage them well, and celebrate their success!

If you've made it this far, congratulations!

Hopefully you've identified some opportunities to improve your marketing by clarifying strategies, evaluating which tactics to use, and adopting new ways to improve your tactical execution, keeping a balance of focus on understanding what to be doing, and doing things well.

As you and your team explore ideas for new marketing programs, think about where they fall in the process, and how they can support your strategy in the marketplace.

Continue learning and improving all of your marketing programs; strive to land in the "best case" scenarios used throughout this guidebook.

Good luck!

To download plans for the activities in this guide, and access a set of "standard operating procedures" for completing each marketing task, visit www.MarketingMO.com.

SHARE
this ebook:

www.ingramcontent.com/pod-product-compliance
Lightning Source LLC
Chambersburg PA
CBHW052051190326
41519CB00002BA/183

9 7 8 0 9 8 8 7 4 3 1 0 6